bush theatre

The Bush Theatre presents
the world premiere of

Our New Girl

by Nancy Harris

12 January – 11 February 2012

Our New Girl

by Nancy Harris

Cast

Richard	**Mark Bazeley**
Annie	**Denise Gough**
Hazel	**Kate Fleetwood**
Daniel	**Jonathan Teale, Jude Willoughby**

Creative Team

Director	**Charlotte Gwinner**
Designer	**Morgan Large**
Lighting Designer	**Hartley T A Kemp**
Composer and Sound Designer	**Elizabeth Purnell**
Assistant Director	**Kirsty Patrick Ward**
Fight Director	**Kate Waters**
Company Stage Manager (on the book)	**Lorna Adamson**
Assistant Stage Manager	**Lizzie Donaghy**
Assistant Stage Manager (placement)	**Alexandra Isaacs**
Production Electrician	**Greg Gould**
Costume Supervisor	**Liz Evans**
Costume Assistant	**Tess Raggett**
Set Builder	**James Turner Inman**
Head of Stage	**Ben Wilkinson**
Casting Director	**Chloe Emmerson**
Chaperone	**Rosemaine Gwilliam**
Kitchen supplied by	**Magnet**

The Bush would like to give particular thanks to: West 12 Centre and UBS, **and would like to thank** Tessa Courtney Bennett, Bose, Mamas and Papas, MacColl Media, John Lewis, HS French Flint and London Luggage.

Mark Bazeley Richard

Theatre includes: *The Seagull* (National Theatre); *Death of a Salesman* (Lyric, West End); *Suddenly Last Summer, Macbeth* (Albery); *Homebody Kabul* (Young Vic); *The Real Thing* (Donmar Warehouse); *Cat on a Hot Tin Roof* (Glasgow Citizens); *Measure for Measure* (Cheek by Jowl/world tour).

Television includes: *The Body Farm, The Accused, Mistresses, Hustle, The Shooting of Thomas Hurndall, Stacked, New Tricks, Spooks, Whistleblowers, Time of Your Life.*

Film includes: *The Special Relationship, The Damned United, Bourne Ultimatum, Noah's Ark, The Queen.*

Kate Fleetwood Hazel

Theatre includes: *London Road, Love's Labour's Lost* (National Theatre); *Life is a Dream, Hecuba* (Donmar Warehouse); *Macbeth* (Tony Nomination for Best Actress: Chichester Festival Theatre/Gielgud Theatre/BAM/Broadway); *Twelfth Night* (Chichester Festival Theatre); *The Winter's Tale, Pericles* (Royal Shakespeare Company); *Othello* (Northampton Theatre Royal); *A Midsummer Night's Dream* (Bristol Old Vic).

Television includes: *A Touch of Cloth, Silent Witness, Waking the Dead, Hustle.*

Film includes: *Harry Potter and the Deathly Hallows: Part 1, Elizabeth: The Golden Age, Vanity Fair.*

Denise Gough Annie

Theatre includes: *The Kindness of Strangers* (Liverpool Everyman); *Ahasverus* (Royal Shakespeare Company); *The Painter* (Arcola); *The Plough and the Stars* (Abbey); *Jesus Hopped the A Train* (Trafalgar Studios); *The Birds* (Gate, Dublin); *Six Characters in Search of an Author* (Chichester Festival Theatre /Gielgud); *As You Like It, By the Bog of Cats* (Wyndhams); *O Go My Man* (Royal Court).

Television includes: *Titanic: Blood and Steel, Waking the Dead, Silent Witness, Messiah, Lie With Me, The Inspector Lynely Mysteries, The Jury, The Bill, Casualty, Holby City.*

Film includes: *The Kid, Robin Hood, Desire.*

Jonathan Teale Daniel

Theatre includes: *Les Misérables* (Queen's, West End); *Oliver!* (Theatre Royal, Drury Lane).

Television includes: an advert for Atlas Editions (Sky Television); a David Suchet documentary (ITV).

Jonathan attends full-time theatre school at Italia Conti Associate School in Clapham.

Jude Willoughby Daniel

Theatre includes: *A Midsummer Night's Dream, Daffodil Scissors* (Italia Conti Associate Theatre).

Television includes: *Annabel's Kitchen* (CITV); a music video for H the City Kid (MTV); and two commercials for LeapPad.

Film includes: *The Piano Player.*

Jude attends Italia Conti Associate School in Clapham.

Charlotte Gwinner Director

Charlotte is an Associate Director at the Bush. Theatre for the Bush includes: *The Knowledge*, *50 Ways to Leave Your Lover*, *Little Dolls*.

She was Director on Attachment at The National Theatre Studio. Other theatre includes: *The Uncertainty Files* (Paines Plough); *Knives and Hens* (Bath Theatre Royal); *The Confederate* (Trafalgar Studios); *Men Should Weep* (Oxford Stage Company/Citizens Theatre); *Riders to the Sea*, *The Shadow of the Glen*, *The Tinker's Wedding*, *Everything Must Go* (Southwark Playhouse); *The Blood of Others* (Arcola); *The Conservatory* (Old Red Lion); *The Country of The Blind* (Gate, London).

Charlotte is also the founder and Artistic Director of ANGLE. She directed *Commercial Rd* and *The Sea at Night* for its inaugural season. Last year, in conjunction with the Bush, Charlotte launched the scheme in West London; the winning plays, *Repentance* and *Behind the Lines*, will run at the Bush for two weeks from 30 January 2012.

Upcoming theatre includes: *Benefactors* (Sheffield Theatres' Michael Frayn Season).

Nancy Harris Writer

Nancy is the Pearson Playwright in Residence at the Bush Theatre, where her previous work includes *Little Dolls* for the Broken Space Season.

Other theatre includes: *No Romance* (Abbey, Dublin); *The Kreutzer Sonata* (Gate, London/La Mama, New York); *Love in a Glass Jar* (Abbey; 20 Love Season).

Radio includes: *Love in a Glass Jar* and *Blood in the Bridal Shop* [co-written with Louise Ramsden for Radio 4]. She has also written for television.

Harley T A Kemp Lighting Designer

Theatre for the Bush includes: *Apologia*, *Wrecks*, *Artefacts* (also New York), *How to Curse*, and the space lighting concept for *The Library*, the initial 2010 season in the Bush's new building.

Other theatre includes: *The Voysey Inheritance*, *Elmina's Kitchen*, *Scenes from the Big Picture* (National Theatre); *Romeo and Juliet*, *The Merry Wives of Windsor*, *Coriolanus*, *The Merchant of Venice* (Royal Shakespeare Company); *Lower Ninth*, *Kiss of the Spider Woman*, *Days of Wine and Roses*, *Passion Play*, *Good* (Donmar Warehouse); *Gaslight*, *As You Like It* (Old Vic); *Mrs Warren's Profession* (Strand); *The York Realist* (English Touring Theatre, Royal Court); *Love, Love, Love* (Paines Plough); *Faith* (Royal Court); *Certain Young Men*, *The Doctor's Dilemma*, *Tongue of a Bird* (Almeida); *The Rubenstein Kiss*

(Hampstead); *The Field* (Tricycle); *Nakamitsu* (Gate, London); *The White Devil*, *The Common Pursuit*, *Total Eclipse* (Menier Chocolate Factory); *The Birthday Party* (Birmingham Rep); *Arcadia*, *The Rivals*, *Loot*, *Paradise Lost*, *The Comedy of Errors*, *The Caretaker* (Bristol Old Vic); *A Number*, *Gladiator Games*, *A Midsummer Night's Dream*, *Original Sin*, *The Tempest*, *Don Juan*, *The Country Wife*, *A View From the Bridge*, *As You Like It*, *Twelfth Night* (Sheffield Theatres); *Rutherford and Son* (Royal Exchange, Manchester); *Where There's a Will* (Theatre Royal Bath Productions); *Treehouses* (Northcott, Exeter); *Dealer's Choice* (Clwyd Teatr Cymru/West Yorkshire Playhouse); *In the Next Room, or the Vibrator Play* (Sydney Theatre Company); *The Gift* (Melbourne Theatre Company); *The Story of Mary MacLane by Herself* (Malthouse Theatre, Melbourne); *Cordelia* (Little Dove Theatre Art, Canberra); *Great Expectations* and *American Buffalo* (Gate, Dublin); *Hysteria* (English Theatre, Frankfurt).

Musical theatre includes: *A Little Night Music* (Walter Kerr, Garrick, Broadway, New York); *Miss Saigon* (Gothenburg Opera); *Showboat*, *West Side Story* (Tiroler Landesteater, Innsbruck); *Promises, Promises* (Sheffield); *The Wizard of Oz* (Birmingham Rep); *Assassins* (Old Fire Station, Oxford).

Opera includes: *Mary Seacole*, *Oreste*, *Oresteia* (Linbury Studio, Royal Opera House); *Les Pêcheurs des Perles*, *Iris* (Opera Holland Park); *M Butterfly*, *Martha*, *The Barber of Seville*, *La Sonnambula*, *Carmen* (Castleward Opera, Northern Ireland).

Hartley is also artistic director of C venues at the Edinburgh Festival Fringe.

Morgan Large Designer

Theatre includes: *Othello*, *Lives in Art* (Sheffield Crucible); *Macbeth* (Singapore Rep, Fort Canning Park); *Midnight Tango* (West End and tour); *Flashdance* (Shaftesbury, West End); *Cat on a Hot Tin Roof* (Olivier Award, Best Revival; Novello, West End); *Footloose* (Novello, West End/tour/South Africa); *Room on the Broom* (worldwide); *The Hostage* (Southwark Playhouse); *Olivier Awards* (2006–2011); *Planet Wonderful* (Royal Danish Ballet); *Dov and Ali*, *Madagascar* (Theatre503).

Upcoming theatre includes: *The Last Horseman* (Madrid) and tours of *The Diary of Anne Frank*, *Monkee Business* and *The Rise and Fall of Little Voice*.

Morgan trained at The Liverpool Institute for Performing Arts.

Kirsty Patrick Ward Assistant Director

Directing credits include: *Four Girls & a Gluten Free Cake* (Old Vic New Voices 24-Hour Plays); *The Baron* (Winner Ignite 4/OVNV); *Present Tense* (Watford Palace); *People Like Us* (OVNV/Vineyard, New York); *Life Support* (York Theatre Royal).

Credits as an associate director include: *Young Pretender* (nabokov, Edinburgh Festival 2011).

Credits as an assistant director include: *50 Ways To Leave Your Lover* (Bush); *The Boy on the Swing* (Arcola); *Bunny* (Fringe First Winner; nabokov, Edinburgh Festival 2010/regional tour 2011).

Kirsty was part of the Old Vic New Voices TS Eliot US/UK Exchange 2011 and was shortlisted for the JMK Young Directors Award 2011.

Elizabeth Purnell Composer and Sound Designer

Elizabeth started writing music for theatre in 1993 when she was resident composer at the Kaos Theatre in Cirencester.

Theatre includes: *Hamlet*, *Treasure Island*, *Woyzeck*, *The Camp*, *Huckleberry Finn*, *The Wills' Girls*, *Robin Hood*, *A Christmas Carol*, *School for Wives* (Tobacco Factory Theatre, Bristol); *Knives in Hens* (Ustinov); *Kindertransport* (Aberystwyth); *The Misanthrope* (Bristol Old Vic); *The Kitchen* (National Theatre); three shows for Angle Theatre (Hackney Empire).

Elizabeth works as an orchestrator for feature film music, and writes music for TV and Radio 4 dramas.

The Bush Theatre

'These are great times for the Bush Theatre... the new building already looks like a winner' Charles Spencer, *Telegraph*

Since its inception in 1972, the Bush Theatre has pursued its singular vision of discovery, risk and entertainment from its home in Shepherds Bush. That vision is valued and embraced by a community of audience and artists radiating out from our distinctive corner of West London across the world. The Bush is a local theatre with an international reputation. From its beginning, the Bush has produced hundreds of groundbreaking premieres, many of them Bush commissions, and hosted guest productions by leading companies and artists from across the world. On any given night, those queuing at the foot of our stairs to take their seats could have travelled from Auckland or popped in from round the corner.

What draws them to the Bush is the promise of a good night out and our proven commitment to launch, from our stage, successive generations of playwrights and artists. Samuel Adamson, David Eldridge, Jonathan Harvey, Catherine Johnson, Tony Kushner, Stephen Poliakoff, Jack Thorne and Victoria Wood (all then unknown) began their careers at the Bush. The unwritten contract between talent and risk is understood by actors who work at the Bush, creating roles in untested new plays. Unique amongst local theatres, the Bush consistently draws actors of the highest reputation and calibre. Joseph Fiennes and Ian Hart recently took leading roles in a first play by an unknown playwright to great critical success. John Simm and Richard Wilson acted in premieres, both of which transferred into the West End. The Bush has won over 100 awards, and developed an enviable reputation for touring its acclaimed productions nationally and internationally.

Audiences and organisations far beyond our stage profit from the risks we take. The value attached to the Bush by other theatres and by the film and television industries is both significant and considerable. The Bush receives more than 3,000 scripts every year, and reads and responds to them all. This is one small part of a comprehensive playwrights' development programme which nurtures the relationship between writer and director, as well as playwright residencies and commissions. Everything that we do to develop playwrights focuses them towards a production on our stage or beyond.

We also run an ambitious education, training and professional development programme, bushfutures, providing opportunities for different sectors of the community and professionals to access the expertise of Bush playwrights, directors, designers, technicians and actors, and to play an active role in influencing the future development of the theatre and its programme. 2009 saw the launch of our new social networking and online publishing website www.bushgreen.org. The site is a great new forum for playwrights and theatre people to meet, share experiences and collaborate. Through this pioneering work, the Bush will reach and connect with new writers and new audiences, and find new plays to stage.

With this season, we have opened the doors of the new Bush Theatre at the Old Shepherds Bush Library. Already, the building feels like it is owned and loved by our audiences and by our artists.

bush theatre

www.bushtheatre.co.uk

At the Bush Theatre

Be there at the beginning

The Bush Theatre would like to say a very special 'Thank You' to the following patrons, corporate sponsors and trusts and foundations, whose valuable contributions continue to help us nurture, develop and present some of the brightest new literary stars and theatre artists.

Lone Star
Gianni Alen-Buckley
Michael Alen-Buckley
Siri & Rob Cope
Jonathan Ford
  & Susannah Herbert
Catherine Johnson
Caryn Mandabach
Miles Morland
Lady Susie Sainsbury
Nicholas & Francesca Whyatt

Handful of Stars
Anonymous
Micaela & Chris Boas
Jim Broadbent
Clyde Cooper
Blake & Michael Daffey
David & Alexandra Emmerson
Catherine Faulks
Chris & Sofia Fenichell
Christopher Hampton
Douglas Kennedy
Mark & Sophie Lewisohn
Adrian & Antonia Lloyd
Mounzer & Beatriz Nasr
Georgia Oetker
Claudia Rossler
Naomi Russell
Eva Sanchez-Ampudia
  & Cyrille Walter
Charles & Emma Sanderson
Joana & Henrik Schliemann
Jon & NoraLee Sedmak
Larus Shields

Rising Stars
Anonymous
Nick Balfour
Tessa Bamford
David Bernstein & Sophie Caruth
Simon Berry
John Bottrill
David Brooks
Maggie Burrows
Clive Butler
Matthew Byam Shaw
Benedetta Cassinelli
Tim & Andrea Clark
Claude & Susie Cochin de Billy
Matthew Cushen
Irene Danilovich
Michael & Marianne de Giorgio
Yvonna Demczynska
Judy Cummins & Karen Doherty
Alexandra Eagle
Ruth East

Charles Emmerson
Jane & David Fletcher
Lady Antonia Fraser
Vivien Goodwin
Sarah Griffin
Hugh & Sarah Grootenhuis
Mr & Mrs Jan Gustafsson
Sarah Hall
Giles Haughton
Hugo & Julia Heath
Roy Hillyard
Urs & Alice Hodler
Bea Hollond
Simon Johnson
Davina & Malcolm Judelson
Paul & Cathy Kafka
Rupert Jolley & Aine Kelly
Tarek & Diala Khlat
Heather Killen
Sue Knox
Neil LaBute
Kirsty Lang
Eugenie White
  & Andrew Loewenthal
Isabella Macpherson
Peter & Bettina Mallinson
Charlie & Polly McAndrew
Michael McCoy
Judith Mellor
Roger Miall
David & Anita Miles
Caro Millington
Pedro & Carole Neuhaus
Kate Pakenham
Mark & Anne Paterson
Julian & Amanda Platt
Radfin Courier Service
Kirsty Raper
Clare Rich
Sarah Richards
Damian Rourke
Karen Scofield & LUCZA
Russ Shaw & Lesley Hill
Brian Smith
Sebastian & Rebecca Speight
Nick Starr
Andrew & Emma Sutcliffe
The Uncertainty Principle
The van Tulleken family
Francois & Arelle von Hurter
Hilary Vyse & Mark Ellis
Trish Wadley
Amanda Waggott
Edward Wild
Peter Wilson-Smith
  & Kat Callo
Alison Winter

Corporate Supporters
Spotlight Supporter
John Lewis, Park Royal

Lightbulb Supporters
AKA
Mozzo Coffee & La Marzocco
Talk Talk

The Bush would also like to thank **Markson Pianos**, **Westfield** and **West 12 Shopping & Leisure Centre** for in-kind support, and **UBS** for their sponsorship of Supporters' evenings.

Trusts and Foundations
The Andrew Lloyd Webber Foundation
The Daisy Trust
The D'Oyly Carte Charitable Trust
EC&O Venues Charitable Trust
The Elizabeth & Gordon Bloor Charitable Foundation
Foundation for Sport and the Arts
Garfield Weston Foundation
Garrick Charitable Trust
The Gatsby Charitable Foundation
The Goldsmiths' Company
The Harold Hyam Wingate Foundation
Jerwood Charitable Foundation
The John Thaw Foundation
The Laurie & Gillian Marsh Charitable Trust
The Leverhulme Trust
The Martin Bowley Charitable Trust
The Hon M J Samuel Charitable Trust
Sir Siegmund Warburg's Voluntary Settlement
The Thistle Trust

OUR NEW GIRL

Nancy Harris

Acknowledgements

My deepest gratitude and appreciation to Charlotte Gwinner, an extraordinary director, collaborator and friend, for all that she gave and gave in bringing this play into being.

I would also like to thank Josie Rourke for her commitment, insight and support throughout the process.

And lastly, my deepest thanks to the following:

Anne Harris, Julia Molony, Robert Coffey, Georgia Fitch, Clare Strong, Nicola Waddell, Niamh O'Sullivan. Alexandra Goddard, Vittoria Colonia, Anthony Weigh, Claire Everett, Rochelle Stevens, Michelle Butterly, Jonathan Humphreys, Mary-Anna Kearney, The Pearson Playwright's Scheme, The Peggy Ramsay Foundation and my family: Eoghan, Connie, Mungo, Aengus, MirKev and Sophie.

Nancy Harris

For Anne

4

Characters

DANIEL, *eight*
HAZEL ROBINSON, *anywhere from thirty-nine to forty-two,
    mother of Daniel, seven months pregnant at the start of the
    play, eight months by the end*
RICHARD ROBINSON, *forties, Daniel's father*
ANNIE, *twenty-eight, the new nanny*

Time

London, present day.

Location

The Robinson's kitchen.

Everything a little too shiny, too bright, nothing homely.

A clock ticks constantly in the background.

*In Act Two, the number of bottles of olive oil in the kitchen
should have increased, perhaps even doubled in number.*

Dialogue

/ indicates an overlap in dialogue.

*[ ] indicates a word or sentence that is not spoken, but conveyed
in the playing.*

…indicates an unfinished or unarticulated thought.

*– indicates a very brief pause or a beat where a thought is
being clarified.*

*This text went to press before the end of rehearsals and so may
differ slightly from the play as performed.*

ACT ONE

One

A darkened kitchen. A sense of night.

DANIEL *is standing in the doorway in his school uniform.
Watching.*

A sliver of light from the hallway lights the room.

In one hand, DANIEL *holds a mirror.*

He walks into the kitchen and places the mirror on the table.

He studies his reflection for a beat.

*He takes off his school blazer and rolls up the sleeves of his
shirt in an 'all business' sort of way that appears far beyond his
years.*

He goes to the cupboard and takes out a small first-aid kit.

*He puts it on the table, opens it and takes out a bottle of Dettol
and some tissue.*

He pours the Dettol onto the tissue.

*He brings his ear up close to the mirror – it is magnified in the
reflection – and he begins to clean it very carefully. He finishes.*

*He drags a chair over to the sideboard where several pristine
silver Sabatier kitchen knives of different shapes and sizes are
displayed on a magnetic knife-holder on the sideboard. They
glint in the light.*

He climbs onto the chair and reaches for one.

He climbs down and goes back to the mirror.

He looks at the reflection of his ear once more.

He takes the knife and slowly begins to lift it towards his ear.

*Suddenly he glances back toward the door as though worried he
is being watched in the darkness.*

Nothing.

He turns back to the mirror again and brings the knife to the top of his ear.

The blade hovers beside the flesh.

He grips his earlobe, closes his eyes and lifts the knife –

Blackout.

Two

Several weeks earlier.

The kitchen table is covered with unopened bottles of olive oil. There are a number of boxes on the floor.

ANNIE *stands in her anorak, a suitcase at her feet.*

HAZEL *stands with a phone in her hand, frustrated.*

HAZEL. I'm not blaming you, obviously I'm not blaming you.

ANNIE. No.

HAZEL. None of this is your fault in any way, shape or /

ANNIE. No /

HAZEL. But the fact is – there's been a mistake. I mean, even with the jet lag and the time-zone differences and all of the other things that might distract a person – it still doesn't make sense.

Beat.

I know my husband.

ANNIE. Of course.

HAZEL. And I can't see how he could've just – not remembered to tell me. About this. You know? It's not like it's a small deal.

ANNIE. No.

HAZEL. You're a whole new person standing in front of me and if there was going to be a whole new person standing in front of me, I think he would've let me know about it, don't you?

ANNIE. Yes.

HAZEL. Yes.

Beat.

ANNIE. It's just – this is the address on the email.

ANNIE *holds out a piece of paper.*

HAZEL. I know that. I know this is the address on the – I see that this is the – and that *is* our address but I think – I really think there must have been a – huge... And I'm sorry, you know because you've come all the way.

ANNIE. Yes.

HAZEL. And that's awful for you and if I were you I'd be very angry with... whoever has caused this mess.

ANNIE. I had to pay for the taxi.

HAZEL. I know. Yes. You said about – that.

ANNIE. They told me someone'd pick me up from the airport. So I waited for an hour but when no one came, I just got in a taxi.

HAZEL. Well, that's terrible. That's really – awful.

ANNIE. I thought I should show some initiative because I had the address and, you know, parents can be busy.

HAZEL. Yes. Well. Tell me about it. My son's finishing school at two and I've a mountain of work to get through and a to-do list as long as my –

ANNIE. It's just – I didn't expect to have to pay for it. The taxi. Out of my own pocket like?

HAZEL. No. No, of course. You shouldn't have to – and I can give you the money. Really, if it's money – that's the least I could... How much was it?

ANNIE. I don't know anyone in London.

HAZEL. Oh.

HAZEL looks at the phone.

I see. Well, that's… hmmn. That is a bit of a [problem] –

ANNIE. It was forty. The taxi.

HAZEL. Right.

HAZEL rustles around and looks for the money. ANNIE continues.

ANNIE. Which I thought was alright – in a way – cos people at home never stop telling me taxis over here cost a fortune. I was worried he might turn around and say two hundred or something.

HAZEL. Well, we're not far from the – airport really.

She gives ANNIE forty pounds.

ANNIE. Thanks.

They look at one another.

HAZEL. It's just I'm just not sure how we [proceed] – you know. Now. I'm not sure where we – go… from here. Is there someone we can ring or – or a head office?

ANNIE. It's in Birmingham.

HAZEL. Birmingham?

ANNIE. The agency is based in Birmingham.

HAZEL. God. Really? Well, that's, no – you might as well go back to Sligo at that rate. It is Sligo, isn't it? That's where you said you're from?

ANNIE. Yes.

HAZEL. Sorry – I don't know Ireland all that [well] – We were supposed to go on our honeymoon.

ANNIE. To Sligo?

HAZEL. No. Ireland – but Richard had an exam so we didn't. Sorry. I'm rambling. I could call him again but that's the fifth time and I'm pretty sure he's probably on a plane. Or a bus. Or asleep. I don't even know what time it is there.

ANNIE. On the phone he said he'd be delayed.

HAZEL. On the... You – spoke to him on the phone?

ANNIE. Yes.

HAZEL. Richard?

ANNIE. Didn't I say that at the start?

HAZEL. No.

ANNIE. Oh. Yes. We spoke a couple of times. To finalise the arrangements.

HAZEL. Finalise the /

ANNIE. He said he was due back today from... Haiti, is it?

HAZEL. Yes.

ANNIE. Where the big earthquake was?

HAZEL. Yes.

ANNIE. Yeah. But there's been an emergency or something so he has to stay on now.

HAZEL. Yes, he's been asked to... So you – spoke to my husband on the phone when he was in Haiti?

ANNIE. I'm hardly just going to go getting on a plane to move to a new country and not have any idea who I'm moving in with, now, am I?

HAZEL. No. Well. No.

ANNIE. That'd be crazy.

HAZEL. Yes.

ANNIE. The agency don't let you do things like that anyway. They're strict. I had to send pictures and references and everything and your husband had to send pictures and references –

HAZEL. References?

ANNIE. Sounds like he does some really wonderful work.

HAZEL. ...Yes.

ANNIE. He sent over a picture of Daniel too.

HAZEL. Daniel?

ANNIE. He's lovely.

HAZEL. Richard sent a picture of – Daniel to you?

ANNIE. He sent a few. That's how I'm sure there hasn't been a mistake. Because you were in one of the pictures too.

HAZEL. Me?

ANNIE. All three of you were. Looked like you were on holidays. Somewhere nice. South of France, maybe?

HAZEL. I'm sorry *you* have a picture of – me… on holiday in… We've never been to the south of France.

ANNIE. Well, it looks like the south of France. The way I'd imagine it. It's a nice picture. You're in a bikini. You're not pregnant in it so it was obviously… a while ago.

HAZEL. No. No, this is too –

HAZEL *presses redial on her phone.*

ANNIE. I have it on my email.

HAZEL *puts the phone to her ear.*

I can show you if you want. It's pretty standard for families to send photographs to girls. He didn't do anything – bad in sending it. Your husband.

HAZEL. No, maybe not but I have to say – I mean – I'm sure you understand this is all just a little bit too – for me – for a Tuesday afternoon – you know? – a picture of me in a bikini in the south of – Fuck it, now it's just going straight to the machine.

She hangs up.

She looks at ANNIE, *a sense of desperation.*

I don't know what to say. I have a whole afternoon's work to – and my son –

ANNIE. Daniel

HAZEL. – finishes at two and to be quite honest this really is the last thing I need to –

ANNIE. Should I go and get him for you?

HAZEL. No, that's – Thank you. No. I just… Exactly – *when* – did you and Richard organise these pictures and references and… things?

ANNIE. Three, four days ago. Maybe. The agency said you needed someone quickly. I said I'd be happy to come as soon as you wanted. Nothing much going on in Sligo, these days.

HAZEL. I just can't believe he would do something like this without telling me.

ANNIE. Maybe he wanted to surprise you.

HAZEL. Surprise me?

ANNIE. He said you were tired.

HAZEL. Tired?

ANNIE. Stressed.

HAZEL. Stressed?

ANNIE. He said you needed some support… Daniel's been a bit of a handful – lately. That's what he said.

HAZEL *stares at her.*

No, please don't be angry. Cos – like he sounded really concerned when I spoke to him. He sounded really worried about you.

HAZEL. Well, he might have voiced his concerns at some point – *before* he organised for a perfect stranger to turn up on my doorstep unannounced.

Beat.

Sorry. That was – I'm… Look, I am completely aware that none of this is your doing, Annie, and as I said I'm absolutely not blaming you for… My husband is a very – headstrong person. And he's a doctor so – you know – there's a whole ego at play. And clearly he has just decided from his hideout in Haiti that he knows what's best for me and his son but in fact the last thing on earth I want is a nanny. You know. I don't need a nanny. Annie.

ANNIE. That's very male, isn't it?

HAZEL. What?

ANNIE. To just want to – fix things. To just find a solution and think that's that now. It's all that Mars, Venus, stuff.

HAZEL. Hmmn.

ANNIE. Have you read that book?

HAZEL. No. I have it on the shelf but… no.

ANNIE. It's good.

HAZEL.… What do people – do in these situations? Normally.

ANNIE. What do you mean?

HAZEL. Do you have a number? For emergencies? Surely, if this agency is so strict about keeping their girls safe, then someone must've given you a number in case, you know – something goes wrong.

ANNIE. They did give me a number.

HAZEL. Oh good.

ANNIE. But it's in Birmingham.

HAZEL. I see.

ANNIE. Everything's done out of Birmingham.

HAZEL. Well, could we put you on a train?

ANNIE. To Birmingham?

HAZEL. To the head office?

ANNIE. I don't think that's allowed.

HAZEL. Why not?

ANNIE. Could I trouble you for a glass of water? The taxi had one of those little air fresheners in it and my throat's gone all –

HAZEL. Oh. Yes. Of course. Sorry I – I should have offered you some – Would you like a cup of –

ANNIE. No.

HAZEL looks at her watch.

HAZEL. Suppose there isn't time.

ANNIE. Water's grand.

HAZEL fills her a glass of water.

ANNIE takes it. She drinks it.

HAZEL looks at her phone.

HAZEL. I realise this must be very disorientating for you.

ANNIE. A bit, yeah.

HAZEL. It's disorientating for me.

ANNIE. It's just – I was looking forward to meeting you all.

HAZEL. Oh.

ANNIE. Your husband seemed like a really decent man on the phone. And you looked like such a lovely family in the pictures. And your house –

HAZEL. The house is a pigsty. That was one of the things on my to-do list – 'clean house'. Never got around to that one. Never do.

ANNIE. Well, sure I'm practically from a pigsty, so don't feel bad on my account.

HAZEL. Sorry?

ANNIE. I was – joking. We have a farm below at home, you know.

HAZEL. Oh. How – nice.

ANNIE. Not my bag really. I've always thought I was a city girl at heart. Here, I just remembered, I've something for Daniel.

She opens her bag.

HAZEL. Oh. Now. You really didn't have to / do that.

ANNIE. It's only small.

She takes out a little bag of plastic farm animals.

HAZEL. God, that's very – hmmmn.

ANNIE. There's everything there, pigs, goats, sheep, a chicken. I mean, he's probably a bit big for it now – he's probably far more interested in computers or what have you but I thought, you know… animals.

HAZEL. He loves animals.

ANNIE. I thought he might.

HAZEL. Thank you.

HAZEL *looks at the animals.*

ANNIE. He has a sweet face in the picture.

HAZEL. Who?

ANNIE. Daniel.

HAZEL. Oh. Yes… This was very kind of you.

She looks at her watch.

Oh God, it's twenty-to, I'm going to have to [go] – If he's out there longer than five minutes they take him into the principal's office and you have to go and get him. It's a whole shaming system – here. Why don't you call someone?

HAZEL *hands the phone to* ANNIE, *starts quickly gathering her things, looking for keys, etc.*

Your family or – or the agency. That's probably the best course of action at this stage, don't you think?

ANNIE *looks at the phone.*

I'm happy to drop you off anywhere. Near a Tube or something. Where are my – I think the trains to Birmingham go from Euston, so that's an option if you – want it. Maybe.

She looks at ANNIE *who is still staring at the phone.*

What do you think?

ANNIE *looks at her.*

God, this really is a horrible mix-up. I'm so sorry – if I'd had any idea, obviously I would've… You know.

ANNIE. The thing is, Hazel – is it alright if I call you Hazel?

HAZEL. Of course. Yes.

ANNIE. You sure?

HAZEL. Absolutely.

ANNIE. Well, the thing is… it's not really been a mix-up, has it?

HAZEL. Well, it has, because I assure you I have never said to my husband that I wanted a nanny. Why would I want a nanny? I work from home now.

ANNIE. Sure /

HAZEL. I might be worked off my – feet but I'm here. I'm always here. I'm here.

ANNIE. Fair point yeah. But still. That's more of a misunderstanding than a mix-up, isn't it?

HAZEL. Well.

ANNIE. Cos like, a mix-up would imply an external error on the part of the agency or myself which has nothing to do with you or your husband and which has led to me flying over here and landing on your doorstep. Which wouldn't be your fault.

HAZEL. No /

ANNIE. But a misunderstanding between you and your husband which led to him calling the agency and booking my flight and faxing a contract which both of us signed agreeing that I would start work today, that sort of… well, that sort of is – your fault. In a way. If you think about it.

HAZEL. Well, it's my husband's fault, yes.

ANNIE. So he should probably take responsibility for it.

HAZEL. Well – yes but he's in Haiti so as usual the responsibility falls to me.

ANNIE. But from the agency's perspective, I've honoured my
end of the bargain. And they've honoured their end of the
bargain.

HAZEL. Of course.

ANNIE. It isn't their fault there's been this misunderstanding.
And it isn't my fault there's been this misunderstanding.

HAZEL. I know that. I said that /

ANNIE. I just want to do my job.

HAZEL. Which is completely fair but –

ANNIE. You said you had a to-do list as long as your arm.

HAZEL. I do but –

ANNIE. So maybe me being here is sort of… a blessing. You
know.

HAZEL. No.

ANNIE. No?

HAZEL. No. Look. Look. I can see that this is a horrible
predicament for you, Annie. You're in a strange city away
from home and you thought there was a job for you. And I
feel utterly utterly terrible that I can't do more to help you
out. But this – really isn't a great time. I've just started up a
new business which I'm sort of learning as I go. My body is
on loan to something that sucks every last nutritional fibre I
put into myself away, my brain is so full of things I have to
do that if I add one more to it, I might internally combust.
And if I don't go and collect my son in the next thirty seconds
I am going to be dealing with a hysterical eight-year-old who
will be throwing various inanimate objects around the room
until midnight when I might finally get a chance to do some
of the work I was supposed to do three weeks ago. So if you
could just tell me where you would like me to drop you or
who you would like to call, that would be brilliant because
one thing is for certain, Annie, I do not need a nanny.

The two women look at one another.

Three

Afternoon. Three days later.

DANIEL *stands at the front of the room reciting.* ANNIE *is at the table making notes in a notepad.*

HAZEL *is struggling with some boxes.*

DANIEL.
    Incy Wincy Spider climbed up the water spout,
    Down came the rain and washed the spider out,
    Out came the sun and…

HAZEL. 'Dried up.'

DANIEL. No.

HAZEL. It's 'dried up'.

    He starts again.

DANIEL.
    Incy Wincy Spider climbed up the water spout,
    Down came the rain and washed the spider out,
    Out came the sun and…

HAZEL. '*Dried up*.' For God's sake, Daniel, no woman over the age of thirty wants to keep repeating that. It's 'dried up'.

DANIEL.
    …dried up all the rain,
    And Incy Wincy Spider climbed up the spout again.

    He turns and looks at ANNIE.

    The end.

    ANNIE *claps*.

ANNIE. Very good.

HAZEL (*to* DANIEL). That's enough now.

HAZEL drops one of the boxes.

Shit.

ANNIE. Oh here, let me give you a –

HAZEL. It's fine.

ANNIE moves to help her, but HAZEL picks the box up quickly.

ANNIE. You really shouldn't be doing that in your condition.

HAZEL. I'm just pregnant, I'm not the Pope. I'm fine – see? Fine.

She goes to put the box on the table but DANIEL is in her way, playing with a toy plane and the plastic farm animals.

(*To* DANIEL.) Could you move those, please? I need the table.

DANIEL *doesn't.*

Now, Daniel. What did I say about toys in the kitchen?

ANNIE. Oh. That's my fault. I said he could.

HAZEL. Well, he can't. I need the – space. He has his own room for this sort of thing.

ANNIE. Come on, Daniel, let's put these somewhere better.

ANNIE helps DANIEL clear the table. She smiles at him tenderly as she does. HAZEL stands, waiting. She looks around at all the boxes. Sighs.

HAZEL. They just keep coming and coming. Every single – I mean. There's even bloody boxes in the new cot now. At this rate there'll be nowhere for a baby to sleep.

DANIEL. You said the baby has its own room.

HAZEL. Yes, I know, but it's filled with crap.

DANIEL. Crap?

HAZEL. Boxes.

DANIEL. You said crap /

HAZEL. Boxes. I haven't got round to painting it yet either. So there's every chance the baby might have to bunk in with you when it comes, Daniel. How would you like that? Sharing your room with the baby?

DANIEL *makes a face and moves off with the last of the animals.*

Well then, don't keep your toys in the kitchen.

ANNIE. I don't mind doing a bit of painting. If it'll help. Like I said, throw anything at me. Whatever makes it – easier.

HAZEL *ignores her and starts to unpack the box.* ANNIE *picks up one of the little bottles of oil.*

(*Reading.*) 'Made in Sicily.' Is this the little town where these are from?

HAZEL. Yes.

ANNIE. So pretty. And all home-made?

HAZEL. It's a little family-run place. Nobody speaks much English, which I thought was fantastic until they started sending – I mean, surely I can't have ordered *all* of these?

ANNIE. Is that where you were in the photograph then? Sicily?

HAZEL. What photograph?

ANNIE. Of you in the bikini. That Richard sent.

HAZEL. Oh. Yes. Must've been.

ANNIE. Not pregnant.

HAZEL. No. Not quite – pregnant. I was still at the firm then.

ANNIE *looks at the oil.*

ANNIE. Wow. Big change, all this. From being a lawyer.

HAZEL. Yes.

HAZEL *picks up some papers – clearly doesn't want to discuss.*

ANNIE. Not exactly an obvious – career move. Law and order to… olive oil?

HAZEL. Well, the world hardly needs more lawyers, does it? A sense of justice might lure you in there but – Where did I put those goddamn barcodes? Every single stockist has a different system, it'd do your head in.

ANNIE *glances at her notepad, flicks through a few pages.*

ANNIE. Well, I only have a few more questions anyway.

HAZEL *does her best to keep busy.*

HAZEL. Hmmmn?

ANNIE. Meat.

HAZEL. Meat?

ANNIE. Does he eat meat?

HAZEL. Of course he – eats meat.

ANNIE. Great. (*Writing.*) What kind of meat?

HAZEL....Um. Sausages.

ANNIE. And?

HAZEL. And sausages.

ANNIE....What about other meat? What about say – a fillet or a chop?

HAZEL. It's just sausages really for the moment.

ANNIE. Right. (*To* DANIEL.) We might have to do something about that, mister.

HAZEL. There's nothing you can do about it. He's a fussy eater. Always has been. Getting anything into him's – He'd chronic colic as a baby. Cried all night for weeks. I had to give up caffeine, dairy, milk, cheese, cabbage. The way the midwives carried on you'd think my breast milk was poisoned.

ANNIE. God.

ANNIE *looks a little awkwardly at the notepad.*

Well, I'm good with pork. Saw my first piglet killed when I was twelve.

DANIEL *stops and looks at* ANNIE *admiringly.*

DANIEL. You saw a piglet get killed?

ANNIE. That probably sounds awful to ye.

HAZEL. No. Not – awful. We know what happens.

ANNIE. His name was Barry.

HAZEL. You named him?

ANNIE. Used name them all. Give them a bit of dignity, my da said. He was into that. If something had to be killed, it had to be honoured. He wasn't so soft on people, sadly. (*To* DANIEL.) He used stun them with a little prod first, then he'd – do the rest. Be over in five minutes. It's only really cruel if you're slow about it.

DANIEL *looks at one of the little toy animals in his hand. It's a pig.*

HAZEL. Like many things, I'm sure.

DANIEL (*holding up the plane*). Look, Annie, the pig is flying the plane.

ANNIE. Wow. Pigs do fly.

DANIEL. NEEEEEEEEEOOOOOOOWWWW.

DANIEL *rushes towards* ANNIE *pretending to fly the plane and knocks into* HAZEL.

HAZEL. Daniel, come on.

ANNIE *winks at him and goes back to her notebook.* DANIEL *carries on 'flying' it.*

ANNIE. Does he get regular sleep?

HAZEL. Well, he sleeps. Every night. That's – regular, isn't it?

ANNIE. What are his usual bedtimes?

DANIEL *grabs one of the bottles off the table and starts flying it too.*

DANIEL. Plane fight /

HAZEL. Daniel, put that back. Now.

> DANIEL *puts it back and smiles at* ANNIE. *She smiles back.*

Sorry – what was the… question?

ANNIE. Bedtimes?

HAZEL. Right. I don't – know. Nine?

> DANIEL *grabs another bottle of oil and 'flies' it across the room.*

DANIEL. NEEEOOOOOOOOOOOOOW /

HAZEL. Come on. Please, I'm trying to count those.

> ANNIE *starts flicking through her notebook.*

ANNIE. Last night he went to bed at ten.

HAZEL (*following* DANIEL). Ten?

> HAZEL *grabs the oil out of* DANIEL*'s hands.*

ANNIE. The night before at eleven-thirty /

HAZEL. Were you –

ANNIE. The night I got here it was almost midnight but he was probably overstimulated.

HAZEL. Have you been – making notes?

ANNIE. Might just help to get things more routine. Calm him down a bit, you know.

HAZEL. Yes, but –

ANNIE. Kids really respond to routine.

HAZEL. Of course but that's not always possible when you're on your own.

ANNIE. Oh I know /

HAZEL. He's very stubborn.

> *While* HAZEL *is talking,* DANIEL *quietly takes the sheets of paper she's been working with and puts them in a drawer.*

I put him to bed and he just comes down. I read him a story and he follows me out. I can't very well spend my whole night hauling him up and down the stairs.

ANNIE. Of course not.

HAZEL. I have things to do. I have all this – to do.

ANNIE. That's why I'm here, isn't it?

Silence.

HAZEL *turns back to the table and sees that her paperwork is missing.*

HAZEL. Where's the delivery note?

ANNIE. Which?

HAZEL. The bit of paper that was just here. It's gone. (*To DANIEL.*) What have you done with it?

He looks at her. Shrugs, carries on flying the plane.

ANNIE. Maybe it fell on the floor.

HAZEL. It's not on the floor. It was here just a moment ago. (*To DANIEL.*) Where is it?

DANIEL. I don't know.

HAZEL. Daniel.

DANIEL. I said I don't know.

HAZEL *begins to search the table frantically.*

HAZEL. For God's sake, that note's got all the quantities –

ANNIE. Here. It might have fallen into one of these /

ANNIE *starts to look through some of the boxes.*

HAZEL. It's the only way I can be sure of what they've sent. They hardly speak a bloody word of –

ANNIE. We'll find it. Maybe it got into one of the cupboards.

HAZEL. Things don't just get into cupboards. People put things into cupboards.

ANNIE *pulls something out of one of the boxes.*

ANNIE. Here. Is this it?

HAZEL *grabs the paper off* ANNIE.

HAZEL. What? No.

DANIEL *starts to circle the room with the plane, quietly going 'vroom'.*

Damnit, Daniel, stop this nonsense and tell me where you've put the bloody papers. Every single time I let you in here I end up losing something.

He ignores her, continues circling.

Daniel! Come on!

Suddenly he rushes at her –

DANIEL. VRRRROOOOOOOM! LOOK OUT /

– and crashes the plane straight into her belly. It drops to the floor.

HAZEL. Ow! /

DANIEL. BOOOOOOOOM! PLANE CRASH! /

HAZEL *doubles over in pain clutching her belly.*

HAZEL. Oh God.

ANNIE. Daniel.

DANIEL. Blood and pig's guts all over the floor.

ANNIE. Daniel, stop. Hazel… Jesus. Are you – okay?

HAZEL *stays doubled over. Doesn't respond.*

ANNIE *looks around, tries to guide her to a chair.*

Here. Why don't you sit? There's a chair just – Hazel?

HAZEL *straightens, shaking her head. Hand on belly.*

HAZEL. It's alright – I'm.

She groans. Pain.

ANNIE. I really think you should sit down.

HAZEL. No – it's. I'm.

HAZEL looks at DANIEL. Sudden fury.

For fuck's sake, what the hell has gotten into you?

She makes to hit him, he ducks away behind ANNIE.

Have you any idea how dangerous that was? Have you any idea what you could've done? Ow. Fuck.

ANNIE. Sit down, Hazel. Please.

Reluctantly, HAZEL *sits.*

ANNIE *turns to* DANIEL *and leans down gently beside him so she is crouching at his level.*

Daniel. There's a baby in there. You understand that, don't you? That there's a baby in Mammy's stomach that's very near ready to come out.

DANIEL *stares at* HAZEL. *Doesn't say anything.*

I know you can't see it now, but that baby has little arms and little feet and little fingernails. That baby even has eyelashes now. And he or she can feel everything we do out here. You could've hurt it doing what you did with that plane. You could have hurt it very badly.

HAZEL. You hurt me.

ANNIE. You wouldn't want to do that, would you? You wouldn't want to hurt a small little baby.

DANIEL *shakes his head.*

Course you wouldn't. Do you want to say you're sorry? To the baby? I think it would like that. Don't you?

ANNIE *looks at* HAZEL, *who doesn't offer anything.*

Go on, Daniel. Tell the baby you're sorry for giving it a scare.

Tentatively DANIEL *begins to move towards* HAZEL, *eyes fixed on her stomach.*

HAZEL *watches. Shifts a little.*

Put your hand on Mammy's tummy –

HAZEL. Well, now /

ANNIE. It's alright, this is good for him. (*To* DANIEL.) Go on.

DANIEL begins to step towards HAZEL.

HAZEL. It's okay. Let's just / [leave it]

ANNIE. Go on, Daniel.

HAZEL. I really don't need him to do that.

ANNIE. He wants to do it. You want to do it, don't you, Daniel?

He nods and reaches out towards HAZEL'*s stomach.*

HAZEL. But /

ANNIE. That's it /

HAZEL. Really it's not /

ANNIE. It's alright /

HAZEL. – necessary.

ANNIE. Go on /

DANIEL touches her stomach – she pushes him away violently.

HAZEL. No. Please. Stop it, Daniel – STOP IT. I DON'T WANT THAT.

Silence.

ANNIE *looks a little shocked.*

ANNIE. It's just it's – good for him to connect to the baby as much as possible at this stage. Really helps them adjust when the time comes.

HAZEL. I – understand that. Yes. Of course – but I think I just need a moment with him – not connecting to the baby. If that's okay. I think I just need a moment… to myself. If that's… alright.

HAZEL rubs her sore stomach.

ANNIE picks the plane off the floor, looks at DANIEL *sympathetically.*

ANNIE. He's shocked himself, I think. Poor thing. They don't know their own strength sometimes. They just get these ideas into their heads and then when it all goes wrong they give themselves a fright. You didn't mean it, did you, Daniel? You didn't mean to hurt anyone?

DANIEL *shakes his head.*

HAZEL *looks at him, a slight softening.*

HAZEL. I... know that. I know he [didn't] – (*To* DANIEL.) I know you didn't mean it. You were just – playing. I... I understand. It's okay.

HAZEL *puts a hand out towards him, tries to smile.*

ANNIE. Do you want to give Mammy a hug and make up?

DANIEL *looks at* HAZEL's *outstretched hand.*

He shakes his head and takes a step back grabbing ANNIE's *hand instead.*

ANNIE *looks at* HAZEL, *a little self-conscious.*

Oh now...

HAZEL. It's alright, I'm used to it.

HAZEL *begins to rise somewhat shakily from the chair.*

ANNIE. Here. Let me get you a cup of something.

HAZEL. I'm okay.

ANNIE. Please.

HAZEL. You're not here to wait on us. That's not part of the contract, is it?

ANNIE. Well, a bit of light housework's –

HAZEL. I'll just get on.

ANNIE. Please. Let me make you some tea. It'll only take a minute.

Beat.

Look, your hands are all shaky and everything.

HAZEL *looks at her hands, relents.*

HAZEL. Alright. Maybe just for a… minute.

ANNIE (*pleased*). Good. What would you like? Herbal, lemon, builders'?

HAZEL. Um. Builders'. Please. With milk. Thank you.

ANNIE. What about a biscuit?

ANNIE *comes over with a tin of biscuits, offers one to* HAZEL.

HAZEL. No.

ANNIE. Go on. Sugar's good for a fright… Go on.

HAZEL *picks out a biscuit,* ANNIE *smiles.*

There you go.

HAZEL (*genuine*). Thank you.

ANNIE. No bother. I like looking after people. It's what I'm good at.

HAZEL *bites into the biscuit, beginning to relax.*

And I only have a few more questions anyway.

HAZEL. More – questions /

ANNIE. Vegetables.

HAZEL. Vegetables?

ANNIE. Does he eat vegetables?

HAZEL.…Of course he eats vegetables.

ANNIE. What kind does he like?

HAZEL. Well /

ANNIE. You don't have to answer now /

HAZEL. He doesn't like any kind.

ANNIE. But he eats them often?

HAZEL. Well, as often as I can –

ANNIE. You don't have to answer now.

HAZEL. It's hard – he's fussy.

ANNIE. You really don't have to answer now. Sit there. Relax.
We'll do it when you've gathered yourself.

ANNIE opens a drawer.

Oh.

HAZEL. What?

She pulls a piece of paper out.

ANNIE. Is this that bit of paper you were looking for?

HAZEL (*taking it*). How did it get in there?

ANNIE. You must have done it by mistake. I put things in mad
places all the time when I'm distracted. Keys. My wallet.
You should see some of the places I've put my wallet. The
freezer one time. Told you it didn't go far.

*ANNIE carries on making tea. HAZEL looks at the note,
then at DANIEL.*

HAZEL.…No.

Four

Evening.

DANIEL *and* ANNIE *are sitting at the table. A plate of carrot
sticks between them.*

ANNIE. What's the capital of Iceland?

DANIEL. Reykjavik.

ANNIE smiles and eats a carrot stick.

ANNIE. What's the capital of Argentina?

DANIEL. Buenos Aires.

ANNIE smiles and eats another carrot stick.

ANNIE. What's the capital of Bulgaria?

DANIEL. Dunno.

ANNIE. Wrong. Your turn.

She pushes the plate towards him.

Go on then, mister.

He takes a carrot stick. Eats it. ANNIE *pats him on the head.*

Faint music, off. ANNIE *goes to the window.*

I can see a man holding a tray with glasses of champagne on it.

DANIEL. Again.

ANNIE. And someone's playing a piano. And there's a lady in a hat… that doesn't suit her colouring at all.

DANIEL. Again, Annie.

ANNIE (*still gazing*).…How many eggs in a dozen?

DANIEL. Twelve.

ANNIE. I'd like to go to that party.

She comes back, eats a carrot stick absently.

You're getting good at this.

DANIEL. What happens when her waters break?

ANNIE. When her waters –

DANIEL. Will there be blood?

ANNIE. No. God. No, there won't be blood.

DANIEL. Sometimes there is. Sometimes there's blood and guts and bits of /

ANNIE. It's just – water from the womb. To say the baby's coming. It's perfectly natural.

DANIEL. It's one of the most excruciating things a woman can go through.

ANNIE. A baby's a beautiful thing.

DANIEL. Not if you have perineal tears.

ANNIE. Perineal – tears?

DANIEL. Then they have to sew you up. Or you can have an episiotomy. Where they make an incision. Helps the baby come out faster.

ANNIE. Right.

DANIEL. I'm supposed to go next door. When the waters break. So Richard can drive Hazel to the hospital. But you're here now so I won't have to.

ANNIE. No. Well. I mean, we'll have to – see what your da – what Richard says when he comes back – because it's down to him really.

DANIEL. He'll want you to stay.

ANNIE. Do you think?

He nods. ANNIE *smiles, then glances out the window.*

If I were you I'd want to go in there. Everyone's having a great old time in there.

DANIEL. I want to stay with you.

ANNIE *squeezes his hand.*

ANNIE. And I want to stay with you.

DANIEL. Is it your turn?

ANNIE. Yes, it's my turn.

DANIEL. Close your eyes.

ANNIE. What are you playing at?

DANIEL. Close your eyes, Annie.

He gets up off the chair and moves to take something out from under the table.

ANNIE *closes her eyes, continues talking pleasantly.*

ANNIE. Your da's coming back tomorrow.

DANIEL. I know.

ANNIE. Your mam's lucky having a doctor for a husband, isn't she? He must be very clever.

DANIEL. He knows everything.

ANNIE smiles. DANIEL puts something on the table. It looks like a glass tank with a little blanket covering it.

ANNIE.... Where did he and your – mam meet?

DANIEL. At school.

ANNIE. That's a long time ago.

DANIEL. Hazel was the best in her class. She won all the prizes.

ANNIE. Did she?

DANIEL. That's why Richard liked her.

ANNIE. Have you always called them by their first names?

DANIEL. Yep.

ANNIE. Why?

DANIEL. It's their names. You can open them now.

ANNIE opens her eyes. Blinks.

A sense she has more questions but then she sees the tank.

ANNIE. What's this? Have you got a pet? Where have you been hiding him?

She moves to lift up the blanket. He stops her.

DANIEL. No, you have to guess.

ANNIE. Guess?

DANIEL. What it is. And if you get it wrong, you eat a carrot stick. And if you get it right, I eat a carrot stick.

ANNIE. Oh, very clever. Alright. Is it... a goldfish?

DANIEL. No.

She eats a carrot stick.

ANNIE. Is it… a frog?

DANIEL. Nope.

She eats another carrot stick.

ANNIE. Is it furry?

DANIEL thinks about this.

DANIEL. A little bit.

ANNIE thinks.

ANNIE. Is it scary?

DANIEL.…A little bit.

ANNIE. It's not a mouse, is it?

He shakes his head. She eats a carrot stick.

She moves her ear to the tank.

I can hear something moving.

DANIEL. It moves.

He smiles. She smiles.

ANNIE. Is it dangerous?

DANIEL. A little bit.

She stops smiling.

ANNIE. Is it poisonous?

DANIEL. A little bit.

ANNIE moves back suddenly.

ANNIE. For God's sake, what the hell is in there, Daniel?

DANIEL puts his hand up to his lips.

DANIEL. Shhhhh. (*Whispers.*) She doesn't let me bring it down here.

ANNIE *decides* DANIEL *is joking.*

ANNIE. Are you having me on?

DANIEL. She's frightened of it.

ANNIE *looks around.*

ANNIE (*lowering her voice*). Who?… Hazel?

DANIEL. I look after it myself.

ANNIE. What do you mean?

DANIEL. No one else does it for me. I do it on my own. That's the deal.

ANNIE. Deal?

DANIEL. You won't tell her that I showed you? It's supposed to be a secret.

ANNIE. But –

DANIEL. Please.

ANNIE. Daniel –

DANIEL (*desperate*). Please. She'll take him away if you do.

ANNIE. No… alright. No, I won't – tell her.

DANIEL. Promise?

ANNIE. I – promise. I won't say a thing. It'll be just – between ourselves.

He smiles at her and picks up the tank.

DANIEL. He doesn't know that I have it.

ANNIE. Who?… Your da?

DANIEL. She told me not to say.

ANNIE. But –

DANIEL. She'll be back in a minute. I better put him back.

DANIEL *carries the tank out of the room.* ANNIE *takes a carrot stick and eats it.*

Five

The next day. Morning.

RICHARD *is showing* ANNIE *some photographs on a digital camera. He is tanned and attractive and has the aura of someone who has been out of the country for a good length of time.*

HAZEL *moves around busily making up lunch boxes, breakfast, etc.*

DANIEL *sits at the table in his school uniform. Watching* RICHARD.

RICHARD. That's the inflatable hospital – exterior.

ANNIE. Wow.

RICHARD. OR's just there on the left.

ANNIE. They look just like big tents.

RICHARD. They are just big tents essentially. This was one of our largest wards. That man there had to have both legs amputated.

HAZEL. Richard.

RICHARD *glances at* DANIEL.

RICHARD. He's alright. Aren't you, Big D?

DANIEL *nods, listening.*

ANNIE. God.

HAZEL. Where have I put the goddamn tinfoil?

ANNIE. It's in the second drawer.

HAZEL. Oh.

HAZEL *retrieves the tinfoil, starts to wrap sandwiches.*

RICHARD. Severe head injuries too but he survived which was very lucky considering what happened.

ANNIE. What happened?

HAZEL. Not before school.

RICHARD (*to* ANNIE). I'll tell you later.

ANNIE. And all these medical staff come from all over, do they?

RICHARD. Some are local like my friend Serge here, some are international, Red Cross, et cetera, and then of course there's me and my team.

ANNIE. And you deal with burns?

RICHARD. We deal with what comes in, Annie. In a situation like this, the main objective was keeping people alive.

Behind them HAZEL *is looking for something else.*

ANNIE. Of course.

RICHARD. But yes, burns is what we're there for. These are some of our nurses. Astonishing women.

ANNIE *leans in attentively as* RICHARD *flicks on.* HAZEL *opens cupboards noisily.*

ANNIE. It's funny – you don't always think about burns in a situation like an earthquake, do you?

RICHARD. Well, no, no one does. Which is why this work is so necessary. Because the thing people forget after a hideous natural disaster are all the hideous human disasters to follow. Riots and lootings and fires. You can't imagine. That's Asha –

ANNIE *covers her mouth at the sight of what's on the camera.*

ANNIE. Oh gosh –

From his position, DANIEL *strains to have a look.*

RICHARD. I did her first grafts a year ago.

ANNIE. The poor woman.

HAZEL, *searching, becomes a little more frantic.*

HAZEL. Anyone seen the /

RICHARD. She survived the quake then an oil lamp turned over inside her tent and – whoosh – whole thing went up in flames – her inside it.

ANNIE. No!

RICHARD. She's magnificent really – given what she's been through. And no self-pity. Not a drop. Just pure courage the whole time.

He shows ANNIE *another picture.* DANIEL *strains to see.*

I tell you, Annie, she could teach us all a thing or two.

He smiles. ANNIE *looks at him in utter admiration.*

HAZEL (*clocking* DANIEL*'s interest*). Okay, can we stop with the picture show, please? I thought we were going to stick to our rule about not doing this kind of thing in front of a certain person?

ANNIE (*snapping to*). Oh – of course.

HAZEL (*to* ANNIE). Have you any idea where the tin opener's / gotten to?

ANNIE. Yes. I put it in the second drawer.

ANNIE *opens the drawer, hands the tin opener to* HAZEL.

HAZEL (*feeling foolish*). Right. Thank you… Can't remember what I wanted it for now.

RICHARD. You must excuse me if I go on, Annie.

ANNIE. No. It's… fascinating.

RICHARD. I just get excited. Been working on this project for eight years now and to see it finally taking off and all the brilliant doctors that want to be involved, it's… But – yes. Back to real life – with a bang. You're being quiet, D. Everything okay?

He rustles DANIEL*'s hair.* DANIEL *nods.*

Good man.

ANNIE. I wanted to be a nurse when I was younger. I'd love to do something like what you do. Someday. I mean, obviously I'm not a – but I'd love to… help. In some way. If I could.

RICHARD. Of course you could.

HAZEL *interrupts, handing lunch boxes to* DANIEL *and one to* RICHARD.

HAZEL. Okay. Lunch boxes. One for you and one for you.

RICHARD *laughs*.

RICHARD. I get a lunch box too, do I?

HAZEL. Only today. Tomorrow I'm back to burning my bra.

DANIEL *opens his lunch box and takes out the sandwiches*.

DANIEL. I don't like these.

HAZEL. Yes, you do. They're the same as yesterday.

DANIEL. No I don't.

HAZEL. Yes you do. Put them back in the box, please.

RICHARD. Hey, mate. Don't knock a woman who makes you lunch. She might never do it again.

DANIEL *throws the sandwiches across the table*.

DANIEL. I don't want these.

HAZEL. They're exactly the same as yesterday.

RICHARD. Hang on a second – I've a present for you.

HAZEL. Me?

RICHARD. Daniel.

HAZEL. Right.

HAZEL *puts* DANIEL's *sandwiches back in the lunch box as* RICHARD *goes to his weekend bag and retrieves a plastic 'duty-free' airport bag*.

He gives it to DANIEL.

RICHARD. See – I didn't forget you.

DANIEL. What is it?

RICHARD. Have a look.

DANIEL *takes out a football.*

Pretty cool, eh? I was thinking we could give it a bit of a kick around the garden when I get back from work. Practise some dribbling. Show the ladies what we're made of. What do you think?

ANNIE (*to* RICHARD). You're not going into work now, are you?

RICHARD. 'Fraid I have to.

ANNIE. But you're just in.

RICHARD. That maybe so, but a Miss Scott Jones of Primrose Hill has booked in for an eye-lift consultation at noon, followed by a girl called Kimberly – who wants to be a TV star but needs several moles removed first. Followed by a slew of housewives with various cosmetic emergencies that they simply *must* speak to me about or none of them will ever be able to leave the house again.

ANNIE. No.

RICHARD. These people.

HAZEL. Pay the bills.

RICHARD. Unfortunately.

ANNIE. And you doing all this charity work for nothing.

RICHARD. Keeps me going, Annie. Otherwise – God, I might end up thinking I'm important.

ANNIE. Well, I hope you're not looking at my face with your surgeon's eye.

RICHARD. Don't mess with perfection, Annie, that's my motto.

ANNIE *laughs, embarrassed.* HAZEL *watches, impatient.*

HAZEL. Are we ready?

ANNIE *rushes over to* DANIEL.

ANNIE. Daniel, come on, let's get your blazer on.

RICHARD (*to* HAZEL). You're going too?

HAZEL. Of course.

RICHARD. Aren't we having – breakfast?

HAZEL. There's no time for breakfast.

RICHARD *looks at all the boxes*.

RICHARD. I thought the whole point of this little – domestic endeavour was to make life easier. Take the weight off.

HAZEL. Well, the weight is on, as you can see. And if I don't get some more stockists by the end of the week, we are going to be stuck with a house full of olive oil for a very long time.

RICHARD. Did she tell you, Annie – how we came to have a house full of olive oil in the first place?

ANNIE. No.

HAZEL. Yes, I did. We went to Sicily.

RICHARD. Did she tell you about her massive girl-crush?

ANNIE. Girl-crush?

HAZEL. Richard /

RICHARD. Full-on love-at-first-sight with a Sicilian woman who ran a local restaurant. Alessandra. Big eyes, big [breasts] –

HAZEL. That's not – she was married. And pregnant –

RICHARD. Yes, you were very taken with that. Kept going on about her 'bloom'.

HAZEL. – and had four kids.

RICHARD. You made us eat there every night so you could watch her.

RICHARD *puts his arms around* HAZEL, *flirtatiously*.

HAZEL. Women often find other women interesting – it's not always about sex.

RICHARD. You were obsessed. (*To* ANNIE.) She was obsessed.

HAZEL. I was impressed. She was very – impressive.

RICHARD. *How* was she impressive?

HAZEL. You know, she had a lot to handle. And they hadn't much. A little olive farm to tend, a restaurant to run – Well, it was actually their house which they opened up for visitors in summer. You ate what they ate. She did everything herself. Cooked everything by hand. And her kids were always nearby. Hanging onto her skirt. Weaving in and out between the tables – bringing bread and wine and helping.

RICHARD. Not always helping /

HAZEL. But she never raised her voice. Not once. Not ever. And they were so sun-kissed and so lively and – Alessandra looked so easy and beatific and round with child –

RICHARD. Like something out of a shampoo ad –

HAZEL. That, yes, I suppose I was –

HAZEL *looks at them a little embarrassed, moves away.*

RICHARD. *Obsessed.* And I tell you, Annie, it was quite the impact cos a year ago it was impossible to drag this one out of the office. They had her tipped for partner.

HAZEL. Richard /

RICHARD. Only three other women in the whole company ever made partner. One of them didn't even have kids.

HAZEL. Which everyone seems to point out.

RICHARD. Then off we go to Sicily, meet this Alessandra and –

HAZEL. Now I'm just your partner. And I'm late.

She goes to give him a perfunctory kiss but RICHARD *holds onto her. Pulls her closer.*

RICHARD. Hey. Hang on, hang on a second here. I was looking forward to some alone time. With my – baby.

HAZEL. With your –

He places his hand on her stomach.

ANNIE, *who is helping* DANIEL, *looks over at them.*

RICHARD. I've waited four whole weeks to feel this stomach. It's gotten big.

HAZEL. I know.

RICHARD. It's very sexy.

HAZEL. It's not very sexy. (*Gently.*) Stop it.

RICHARD. It is.

HAZEL. It really – isn't, / Richard.

He mouths at her, 'You're very sexy.'

HAZEL *smiles, a little self-conscious, glances at* ANNIE, *who is very aware of them.*

I've to drop them to school.

RICHARD. Annie can do that. Come on. I've been looking forward to seeing you… I flew through the night for you and everything.

HAZEL. For me?

He mouths 'I want to fuck you' to HAZEL. ANNIE *glances away, uncomfortable, she starts to fuss – putting* DANIEL'*s satchel on his back.*

RICHARD. You know?

ANNIE (*deliberate*). Have you got everything there now, Daniel?

RICHARD *kisses* HAZEL'*s neck.*

RICHARD. What do you say to that?

HAZEL. I don't know what to say to – that. Richard.

RICHARD. Of course you do /

HAZEL. You can't just come in here and /

RICHARD. Let Annie do the driving. Me you and the – bump can have a bit of – family time. Alone. By ourselves.

RICHARD *keeps kissing* HAZEL. *She begins to kiss back.*

Wouldn't you say we've earned that? Hmmm?

Awkward beat as ANNIE *and* DANIEL *watch this.*

ANNIE *coughs, loudly.*

ANNIE. Em… well. Yeah. I mean – I *could* always drive and that's – although we still haven't gotten round to insuring me on the car – so that might potentially be a bit of a problem – with the whole driving thing?

HAZEL *breaks away from* RICHARD *and moves around officiously.*

HAZEL. No, of course you can't drive. Richard. Please. Let's just – stick to the plan. We've all got things to be getting on with.

RICHARD *steps back, disappointed.*

RICHARD. Oh yes. God forbid Ms Scott Jones' eyes aren't lifted by lunchtime.

HAZEL. Annie, shopping list. And there's a bit of ironing for when you're back.

A beat of hesitation as ANNIE *takes the list from* HAZEL.

You said a bit of light housework was –

ANNIE. Fine. Yeah. Fine.

ANNIE *moves away.* RICHARD *rustles* DANIEL's *hair.*

RICHARD. See you later then, big guy. Looking forward to kick-off.

HAZEL *holds out the lunch box.* DANIEL *shakes his head.*

DANIEL. I don't want them.

HAZEL. They're exactly the same as yesterday, Daniel.

DANIEL. Annie made them yesterday.

He walks past HAZEL *and out the door, leaving the lunch box.*

HAZEL (*a little deflated*). We should go.

RICHARD. Go, go. What do I want to see my wife for? It's only been four weeks.

HAZEL *kisses him.*

We'll finish this later.

HAZEL *smiles and leaves,* ANNIE *following. Just before she reaches the door,* ANNIE *hangs back.*

ANNIE....It's – nice to finally meet you. In the flesh, you know.

RICHARD. Yes. Yes. You too. Annie.

ANNIE. Everything's been – good while you've been gone. Just so you know. Everything's been… Nothing to – worry about at all, really.

RICHARD. Oh. Good. Yes. I'm glad.

He takes a sip of his coffee.

ANNIE *stays for a tiny beat longer, then follows* HAZEL *out.*

Six

Evening. Some days later.

There are more boxes and bottles of oil in the kitchen.

The evidence of HAZEL's *business all around too, laptops, folders, etc.*

RICHARD *and* HAZEL *are in the middle of a heated conversation.*

ANNIE *watches from the sidelines.*

RICHARD. For God's sake.

HAZEL. It's alright.

RICHARD. Staring?

HAZEL. That's what they –

RICHARD. Inappropriate staring?

HAZEL. – said. Yes.

RICHARD. Not hitting or bullying or name-calling –

HAZEL. Not this time, no.

RICHARD. But staring?

HAZEL. It was aggressive, they said.

RICHARD. Aggressive staring.

HAZEL. He tried to touch her. She – she thought he was going to do something to her face.

RICHARD. She *thought* he was going to do something to her face?

HAZEL. Yes.

RICHARD. And *was* he going to do something to her face?

ANNIE. No.

    HAZEL and RICHARD look at ANNIE, surprised at the intervention.

    He says he wasn't, no.

RICHARD (*taking out his phone*). I'm calling them.

HAZEL. There's no need to call them now. I've handled it.

RICHARD. It's utterly outrageous.

ANNIE. She's sensitive, you see. The little girl. He scared her.

RICHARD. Scared her how exactly? By looking at her?

ANNIE. I tried to explain that he wouldn't have meant it. I said that I've been here a fortnight and he's been good as gold for the most part. And that even if he did – stare at her a bit too much or – whatever. He wouldn't have meant anything by it.

RICHARD. Of course he bloody wouldn't.

ANNIE. But they wanted to speak to a parent.

HAZEL. And they spoke to a parent. It's dealt with. We don't
need a mediation, Richard.

ANNIE (*to* RICHARD). It's just they wanted an apology.

RICHARD. What?

ANNIE. And obviously that wasn't my place, so…

RICHARD. They wanted an apology?

ANNIE. She's new, the little girl. She's from China. Only been
here a few weeks and they didn't want her to think it was –
cultural.

RICHARD. 'Cultural'?

ANNIE. The staring.

RICHARD. What do they mean by 'cultural'? Are they calling
him a racist?

HAZEL. He made her feel uncomfortable, Richard.

RICHARD. Well, that's her problem, isn't it? I mean, if this
were a court of law or a legal case, Hazel, that would be her
problem, not Daniel's who for all intents and purposes hasn't
actually – done anything? Hmm? Wouldn't it?

HAZEL. Look, can we just drop it.

RICHARD. I hope you told them to go and take a flying leap
off something very high onto something very painful.

HAZEL. Not exactly.

RICHARD. Well, what did you do?

HAZEL. I apologised.

RICHARD. What?

HAZEL. And then I had him apologise.

RICHARD.… You had our son apologise for staring?

HAZEL. She's a little girl from another country. He upset her.
The headmistress was involved.

RICHARD. So you just –

HAZEL. Yes.

RICHARD. Even though he says he didn't do anything?

HAZEL. Well, of course he says he didn't do anything.
Children lie. He was covering his back.

RICHARD. He could have been telling the truth.

HAZEL. It was obvious that he did do something, Richard. I'm
with him all the time. I know what he's like.

HAZEL *turns to the laptop, begins to busy herself.*

RICHARD *looks around, clearly not ready to let it go.*

RICHARD. Annie, what do you think?

ANNIE. What?

HAZEL. Richard.

RICHARD. I'm just asking her opinion. She's the one who had
to call you.

ANNIE. I should have handled this myself, shouldn't I?

RICHARD. You handled it magnificently.

ANNIE (*to* HAZEL). You're far too busy for this.

RICHARD. No she's not. I'm just – wondering what you think,
that's all. As the expert.

ANNIE. Hardly the – expert /

RICHARD. You know what I mean. Should we really be
making him apologise for something he says he didn't do? Is
that really – fair?

ANNIE.... Well, I suppose... I suppose – personally I would
think it's important to give Daniel the benefit of the doubt.

RICHARD. Yes. So would I. Thank you.

ANNIE. So he knows you're on his side. He was so worried *you'd* be angry with him. We went to the shops after school and he didn't let go of my hand once. Just – clung to me like a little mussel the whole time.

HAZEL. The headmistress summoned me in there, Richard.

RICHARD. So what?

HAZEL. So you're not the one who has to face them. You're not the one who has to explain every single time he does something.

RICHARD. Well, I would if you'd let me /

HAZEL. You don't see how they look at me.

RICHARD. Hazel, you've handled emergency injunctions – who cares how some headmistress looks at you?

HAZEL. I care.

RICHARD. Why?

HAZEL. *Because* I care… What do you want me to have done?

RICHARD. Stand up for our son, quite frankly. Protect him from that bunch of screaming harpies that run that precious little –

> DANIEL *enters with a toy plane*. RICHARD *catches himself*.

Hey, hey there, Big D. What are you up to?

> DANIEL *shrugs*. RICHARD *points to the plane*.

Oh, very cool. Very. I'm taking one of those this weekend. To Paris.

HAZEL. Paris?

RICHARD. Just for the night, for that conference.

> DANIEL *watches the two of them closely throughout the following exchange*.

HAZEL. What conference?

RICHARD. I told you. For the fund-raiser. Building
   international interest –

ANNIE. Oh, that journalist rang again /

RICHARD. Yes, thanks, Annie.

ANNIE. From the TV company. Four o'clock tomorrow at the –

RICHARD. She got me on the mobile, thanks.

ANNIE. They're only thrilled to have someone so photogenic,
   she said. Cos most people who do charity work – aren't. Or
   something. I think that was her gist.

   RICHARD *glances at* HAZEL *a little self-consciously.*

RICHARD. It's publicity, Hazel. Badly needed. Funding's a
   disaster.

HAZEL. I see.

RICHARD. These *are* people's lives, you know.

HAZEL. Oh, I know that, Richard. I'm keenly aware of the fact
   that one of us would have to lose a – limb or something in
   this house to get you to stick around.

   DANIEL *looks at* RICHARD *for a beat.*

RICHARD. That's not fair.

HAZEL. Isn't it?

RICHARD. No.

   RICHARD *sees* DANIEL *moving off with the plane.*

   Hey hey – hang on there, big guy. We were hoping to have a
   little word with you. We um – we heard that you were in a
   spot of bother at school today. And we're not angry, we're
   not upset or anything like that – we just want to know if you
   are – upset. By anything the teachers said.

DANIEL. I didn't do anything.

RICHARD. Of course not. Yeah, we know that. We know you
   didn't – do anything to –

ANNIE. Mia.

RICHARD. Or if you did, we know you didn't mean to.

ANNIE. She's shy, isn't she?

RICHARD. Yes, she – It made her feel odd, which is – a bit odd really. But no one's blaming her. She's entitled to her feelings. And so are you. And the thing you'll come to understand about girls, D, is that sometimes they like you looking at them and sometimes they don't. And sometimes it's hard to know which to do because they can bite your head off either way. 'Did you see my new skirt?' – 'No.' Bam! Wrong answer. You know?

He laughs. He stops. HAZEL *is staring at him.*

I'm just trying to explain.

HAZEL. What exactly?

RICHARD. That we're on his side. Mate, I know what it's like being in places where people look different, alright? I'm in places all the time where people look different. It's interesting. It's beautiful. All the diversity in the world. Of course you want to look at it, but these days, looking, it's –

DANIEL. I said sorry.

RICHARD. Yeah, no. We know you said sorry – and that was what they wanted – but it's not what we want. It's not about being sorry, it's about what you did. And I'm trying to say it's okay.

HAZEL. It is not okay.

RICHARD. Hazel.

HAZEL. It is not okay. What Richard is trying to say, Daniel, is that touching someone without their permission is wrong.

DANIEL *looks at* HAZEL.

RICHARD. But *wanting* to touch is not wrong.

DANIEL *looks at* RICHARD.

HAZEL. It is if it makes people unhappy.

DANIEL *looks at* HAZEL.

RICHARD. Making people happy is not our job.

DANIEL *looks at* RICHARD.

HAZEL. We have to respect other people's feelings.

DANIEL *looks at* HAZEL.

RICHARD. While understanding that we might not have
intended to upset them.

DANIEL *looks at* RICHARD.

While accepting that we all have desires and interests that
might not fit in with everyone else's desires and interests, but
that doesn't mean that having them is wrong.

HAZEL. Yesterday a total stranger walked up to me and put his
hand on my belly. Out of nowhere. Happens all the time.
People think it's their right because I'm pregnant. But it's not
their right. It's my stomach and it's their hands.

RICHARD. You're confusing the matter, Hazel.

HAZEL. It's an issue of violation. It's an issue of one person
touching another and the other person not wanting to be
touched.

RICHARD. Okay, yes, but /

HAZEL. And the fact remains that somehow, Daniel, you have
upset a little girl so sufficiently the headmistress is involved.
All I am asking is that you don't do it again. Next time you
get the urge to touch her – or or stare at her – or anyone else
for that matter – sit on your hands, or look at a book, or leave
the room but please don't bother that poor creature, her
nerves can't take it and neither to be frank with you can
mine. Okay?

DANIEL *nods*.

Good.

DANIEL *grabs whatever he came in for and leaves the
room,* RICHARD *half-following*.

RICHARD. Mate, hang on! Daniel! Daniel!

But DANIEL *is too fast.* RICHARD *looks at* HAZEL, *who is back on the laptop.*

HAZEL. They've sent me the wrong bloody quantities. It's a complete mess. I knew this wasn't right. I knew I didn't order all this.

RICHARD. What was that?

HAZEL. What?

RICHARD. 'Sit on your hands.'

ANNIE (*to* HAZEL). I really don't think he meant any harm.

HAZEL. Yes he did, Annie. I know what he's like.

RICHARD. Oh, come on /

HAZEL. People need to be kept in check, Richard.

RICHARD. People?

HAZEL. Children. He needs discipline, he needs – rules, otherwise… he's been extremely difficult lately, you know that.

RICHARD. That may be so but –

HAZEL. The nuances of which Haitian or French or Chinese nurse you find fascinating to look at on your travels are of no relevance to our son.

RICHARD *laughs.*

RICHARD. For God's sake, Hazel, this has nothing to do with – don't twist and turn this into some little paranoid – delusional… This is not about that, this is about –

HAZEL. This is about manners. And I'm trying to make sure our child has some. There is nothing to debate.

HAZEL *turns back to her things, a little rattled.*

RICHARD *watches her. Then turns to* ANNIE.

RICHARD.…Annie. Would you agree with that?

Seven

Night. Very late.

The room is in darkness.

The clock ticks in the background.

HAZEL *enters in a nightdress, holding her bump. She seems tense, anxious, breathing heavily. She pours herself a glass of water and gulps it down.*

She fills it up again and looks around at all the boxes in the kitchen. A sense that she is overwhelmed.

She opens a cupboard and takes out a small overnight bag. She starts to take things out of it somewhat furiously. Nappies, blankets, towels.

Suddenly she stops. A sense that someone is watching.

HAZEL *(calling)*....Hello?... Is – someone... hello?

 A light flashes from under the table. She jumps.

 DANIEL *is sitting under the table holding* RICHARD*'s camera.*

 Oh, for God's sake. Daniel. What are you – doing under there? Why aren't you in bed?

 He doesn't move. She leans down.

 You haven't brought that – thing down here, have you?

 He shakes his head.

 What have you got there?

DANIEL. Nothing.

 DANIEL *puts the camera behind his back.*

HAZEL. Is that what I think it is?

DANIEL. No.

HAZEL. Is that Richard's camera?

DANIEL. No.

HAZEL. Give it to me.

She puts out her hand. He doesn't hand it over.

Now, Daniel.

He doesn't move.

You are not to look at those pictures. How many times do I have to say it? Give it to me. Give. It. To. Me.

He doesn't move. She stands up.

Fine. Have it your way.

She carries on unpacking the bag. DANIEL *watches her from under the table.*

DANIEL. What are you doing?

HAZEL. None of your business.

DANIEL. Where are you going?

HAZEL. None of your business.

DANIEL. Are you running away?

HAZEL. I can't run away. How can I run away? – I'm checking my bag for the hospital. I'm making sure it's all ready.

DANIEL *climbs out from under the table.*

DANIEL. Why are you doing it now?

HAZEL. Because I can't sleep now. And in six weeks there'll be a baby and I won't sleep then. I won't be able to do anything then, so –

DANIEL. Is it coming?

HAZEL. Not this minute.

DANIEL. When?

HAZEL. When it's ready. When I'm ready. When Richard's in the country for longer than five bloody / minutes.

DANIEL. Annie said a baby can come any time it wants.

HAZEL suddenly – violently – snatches the camera out of DANIEL's hand.

HAZEL. You are not allowed to take this camera. Do you understand?

She begins to shake him.

You are not allowed to see these pictures. Do you understand?

DANIEL. Ow! /

HAZEL. When I tell you not to do something, you *don't* do it.

DANIEL. Stop /

HAZEL. When I tell you to behave, you behave. Do you understand? Do you, Daniel? Do you understand?

DANIEL. I want Annie.

HAZEL. 'I want – I want – I want' – I DON'T CARE WHAT YOU WANT.

Silence.

She stops. She releases her grip.

A sense of quiet despair.

…Why are you doing this to me?

She looks at the camera again, gathers herself.

(*Trying.*) These pictures are of very sick people, Daniel. People who have had terrible things happen to them. People – Richard has to help. You do not need to see these pictures.

DANIEL. It was on the table.

She starts to flick through some of the pictures, grimacing.

HAZEL. Oh God. No wonder you won't sleep.

DANIEL. He forgot to take it with him when he left.

HAZEL. How many of these did you look at?

She puts her hand over her mouth at one of the pictures.

I'm not – having these in my kitchen.

She goes to put the camera in the bin but stops herself. She looks around.

I don't want these just – lying around the house. This is a house with a child in it. Am I the only one who seems to give a damn?

She pulls out a chair and drags it over to a shelf.

Here. Hold – this.

She climbs up. DANIEL *stays where he is.*

Daniel, hold this chair and make sure I don't fall.

Very slowly he comes towards her and puts his hand on the back of chair.

HAZEL *straightens, a little unsteady.*

She looks at him, perhaps a tiny bit uncertain of what he might do.

She reaches up to place the camera on the highest shelf. It is a vulnerable position. She has to stand on tiptoes.

As she does, she glances down at DANIEL.

Hold it still now, won't you?

Beat.

Daniel? You will – hold it still?

Beat.

…Daniel?

He nods.

She reaches up and places the camera on top of the cupboard.

There. Now. Better.

She climbs down from the chair. Pushes it back. DANIEL watches.

Go to bed please.

DANIEL *doesn't move.* HAZEL *goes back to the hospital bag.*

Why are you looking at me like that? I said go to bed.

DANIEL *keeps watching. He's getting to her.*

What – Daniel? What are you looking at?

DANIEL *doesn't move.*

Are you trying to drive me completely – Do you have any idea what it's like not to have even one moment to yourself? Ever? Do you? Why are you looking at me? What is it? What? What? *What* do you see?

She stops and sits down on a nearby chair, upset.

She closes her eyes.

She takes a breath.

She opens them.

He watches her the whole time.

Suddenly she leans forwards towards him and whispers.

Would you like to have pushed that chair – is that it?…The one that I was standing on – would you like to have – pushed it? Would you like to have pushed me?

DANIEL *doesn't respond.*

Is that what you think I deserve?

She puts a hand to her forehead, aware her tiredness has got the better of her.

Go to bed, Daniel.

DANIEL. I want to sleep in your room.

HAZEL. No.

DANIEL. Please.

HAZEL. You're too big and I'm too pregnant.

DANIEL. Please.

HAZEL. I can't, Daniel. I just –

She looks at him, a sense of defeat.

– can't.

Beat.

Go to bed.

Beat.

DANIEL.…Annie writes in a notebook.

HAZEL. I know that.

DANIEL. All the time.

HAZEL. I know.

DANIEL. What does she write about?

HAZEL. I have no idea. I have absolutely no idea what Annie writes about in her little bloody notebook. All the time. Please, Daniel. Go away.

She looks at him, pleading.

I'm so tired. I'm so. Please. Just once – just – do as I ask.

Beat.

DANIEL.…I think she writes about you.

They look at one another.

Fade.

ACT TWO

Eight

The Robinson's kitchen. A week later. Evening. Boxes everywhere.

Lights up on RICHARD *holding a glass tank with a large black spider in it, up towards the light.*

HAZEL *sits with a phone in her hand.* ANNIE *stands, with her back to the tank, unable to look at the spider.*

ANNIE. I'm so sorry.

RICHARD. Please don't apologise.

ANNIE. But I think you had a right to know /

RICHARD. Of course I had a right to know.

ANNIE *glances around at* DANIEL.

ANNIE. I'm sorry, Daniel.

RICHARD. *You* have nothing to be sorry for, Annie.

ANNIE (*to* DANIEL). But he's your da. You can't keep something like this a secret from your da.

RICHARD. What on earth were you doing, Hazel?

HAZEL. It's not what you think.

RICHARD *looks inside the tank.*

RICHARD. It's a tarantula. The size of my bloody fist. That I had no idea was here. I mean, look at this thing.

RICHARD *holds the tank out towards* HAZEL. *She moves away.*

HAZEL. I – can't look at it.

RICHARD. Well, if you can't look at it why the hell did you buy it?

ANNIE. I just couldn't bear the idea of something like that in the house without you knowing. I mean – what if it escaped or something?

RICHARD. Well, exactly.

ANNIE. I kept having visions of it crawling across my face in the middle of the night. Or getting into my bed and making a nest in my hair. I woke up one morning and I swear I could see it just lying there beside me on the pillow.

She shudders.

HAZEL (*to* ANNIE). I thought you grew up on a farm.

RICHARD. What's that got to do with anything?

HAZEL. I just didn't know she was so delicate – she's happy to watch baby piglets being slaughtered.

ANNIE. *That's* a poisonous insect.

DANIEL. It's not an insect. Insects have six legs.

RICHARD. Well, yes that's – right actually. Very good, D.

HAZEL. And it isn't poisonous.

ANNIE. How do you know?

HAZEL. The man in the shop told us.

ANNIE. And you believe him? Those things bite. You're going to have a newborn baby here soon, I mean, if that got out and – God forbid – did something –

HAZEL. It's not going to get out.

ANNIE. Well, you hear those stories about pets and little babies –

HAZEL. But it's not going to – it's in a tank – it can't – that makes no sense.

RICHARD. What makes no sense is that you would have bought a spider for our son and told him to hide it in his room.

DANIEL (*to* HAZEL). Annie said she wouldn't tell.

RICHARD (*to* DANIEL). *Annie* shouldn't have been put in that position. I mean, God, Hazel, telling a child to keep secrets – what does that open him up to?

HAZEL (*flustered*). I wasn't trying to – I didn't mean to – I just thought… He – wanted a pet. I knew you wouldn't approve.

RICHARD. Of course I wouldn't approve. The way you've been lately – I would have said you've enough on your plate. I mean, it's a fucking arachnid, it should be in the jungles of Brazil or somewhere – not… Most people buy kittens.

HAZEL. He didn't want a kitten. I can't always be the – bad guy. Sometimes I have to give in.

RICHARD (*to* DANIEL). I'm sorry, mate, but this thing can't stay in the house.

DANIEL (*re* HAZEL). But *she* said –

HAZEL. Richard.

RICHARD. You're terrified of it. Annie's terrified of it. He's terrified of it.

DANIEL. I'm not /

RICHARD. It's not a sensible pet. This should have been a family decision. I should have been consulted.

HAZEL. You weren't here to consult.

RICHARD. That's not the point.

HAZEL. I wasn't consulted about Annie. She just showed up at our door.

RICHARD. Hazel.

ANNIE. With all due respect, Hazel, I – I think they're two very different matters. *He* was only trying to help you.

Both RICHARD *and* HAZEL *look at* ANNIE. *Uncomfortable*. RICHARD *points to the tank*.

RICHARD. Now look, that's. Let's – just focus on the matter at hand. How long do these – things actually live?

DANIEL. Ten years. Sometimes twenty. If you look after them.

RICHARD. Oh God, no. Sorry, Daniel. No. Okay. We're going to have to find him a new home.

DANIEL. Where?

RICHARD. I don't know. Maybe – you can bring it back to the shop?

HAZEL. They don't take them back.

RICHARD. What?

HAZEL. He said so when we bought it. 'No returns.'

RICHARD. Of course 'no returns'. Very fucking clever. Some – yummy mummy all pearls and perfume – comes into a pet shop with her son, asks to buy a spider – that she can't even look at – of course he says 'no returns'. He's a tradesman not an idiot. He wants to make a profit.

DANIEL (*to* HAZEL). I don't want to give it back.

RICHARD. Of course you don't, mate.

DANIEL (*to* HAZEL). I looked after it myself.

RICHARD *looks at* DANIEL, *softens*.

RICHARD. Look, maybe – maybe we can take it to the zoo. See if they can put it somewhere in the – reptile house or – whatever – or maybe we can take it up to Hampstead Heath, release it back to the wild.

HAZEL. You can't release a tarantula on Hampstead Heath.

RICHARD. Why not?

HAZEL. It's not from there.

He holds the tank towards HAZEL *again, she flinches*.

RICHARD. It's not from anywhere near here. It's from the rainforest. Why on earth would you buy him something that you have a mortal fear of?

HAZEL. I didn't /

RICHARD. What's the reasoning there, Hazel? Talk me through it /

HAZEL. I was trying to /

RICHARD. Yes?

HAZEL. I was trying to teach him responsibility.

RICHARD *laughs*.

RICHARD. You were trying to teach him responsibility by
buying him a pet and telling him not to tell his father. That's
great. That's – brilliant. That's responsibility right there.

HAZEL. You don't understand.

RICHARD. What don't I understand?

HAZEL. You were away. He wasn't sleeping. The baby had me
up all night.

RICHARD. Okay, fine.

HAZEL. No you don't –

RICHARD. I get it.

HAZEL. I couldn't –

RICHARD. Cope, yes –

HAZEL. No.

RICHARD. I get it, Hazel. I know the story by heart. We've
been around the block with this one.

Suddenly –

HAZEL. He wanted something to look after. He asked for
something to take care of – that is, after all, what a pet is,
something to take care of. And yes, alright, it is a strange
thing from a strange place and I'm scared of it – but he
wanted it. It was the only thing that seemed to interest him
and – I thought… I thought maybe it would be a good idea.

RICHARD. 'Maybe it would be a good idea'? Jesus /

HAZEL. Sometimes we have to take care of things we're
frightened of. Sometimes we're stuck with things that we
don't like. These are life skills. How do you know you have
what it takes? There's no preparation. You can't know you're

up to the job of taking care of something until that thing is in
front of you and it lives or dies. That's the only way to really
– test. So I thought, okay. You want it. Go on. Let's. Do this.
You know. Let's see if you can look after this. Let's see. And
it turns out. Well, it turns out actually… that he can.

RICHARD *looks at* HAZEL, *the fizz of shock.*

RICHARD. O-kay… You know I'm wondering if we can find
some sort of – solution to all this. That we can just sort of
thrash out here and now. Because I've got to write a speech
for this fund-raiser tomorrow – which is pretty important to
me, believe it or not, and I don't actually have all night to
stare into a glass tank at something whose legs are as thick as
my fingers. Daniel, what's say you and I get up early and go
to the zoo and see if we can find this fella a home?

DANIEL. I want to keep him.

RICHARD. Well, I'm afraid that's not possible.

DANIEL (*to* HAZEL). You said /

HAZEL. I said if he stayed in your room.

RICHARD. Yes, okay. We know that Hazel got him and Hazel
said you could keep him and all of that. But Hazel only said
that because… she's tired. Isn't that right, Hazel?

HAZEL *doesn't say anything.*

Hazel only bought this because she is having a baby and
there are a lot of hormones in her body and she didn't –
completely think it through. Isn't that right, Hazel?

HAZEL *doesn't say anything.*

We don't keep secrets here. We don't tell each other not to
tell things. That's not right. That only happened because
Hazel's been under stress and she needed help and she
thought this was the right thing to do. Isn't that right, Hazel –
help me out here, for God's sake.

Beat.

HAZEL *looks at* DANIEL.

HAZEL.… Yes. That's right.

RICHARD. But now that Annie's here and now that I'm home, it's quite clear that this fella can't stay any more. And I know that's disappointing but that's the way it is.

DANIEL (*to* HAZEL). I don't want to give him back.

HAZEL *looks away.*

(*To* ANNIE.) I don't want to give him back.

ANNIE. If your da says you have to.

RICHARD. I do. And I know it's not fair, D, but there's no other way round this. I'm putting my foot down.

RICHARD *picks up the tank.*

Now. Let's put him back upstairs and you can say goodnight and goodbye properly and then – bugger.

He knocks against one of the boxes.

I thought you were sending these back.

HAZEL. I've been trying to call Alessandra, no one's picking – up.

RICHARD. How can one little olive farm produce this much oil?

HAZEL. They've just messed up the numbers.

RICHARD. Or they've sent you everything they couldn't flog for the last five years. I swear, Hazel, girl-crush or no girl-crush, I'm starting to think these people see you coming.

HAZEL. I'll try again.

HAZEL *starts to dial a number.*

DANIEL. I don't want to give him back.

ANNIE. It'll be alright, pet. We'll find him a good home. He'll be happier.

She puts her arms out to hug him –

I promise.

– but he walks away from her towards HAZEL.

DANIEL. I don't want to give him back.

HAZEL. There's nothing I can do about it. You heard what they said.

RICHARD *waits at the door with the tank.*

RICHARD. Daniel, mate. Let's go.

DANIEL *keeps staring at* HAZEL, *who is becoming unnerved.*

HAZEL. There's nothing more I can do for you. You *heard* them, Daniel. You heard. It's completely out of my hands.

She turns her back on him quickly and puts the phone to her ear.

He keeps staring.

Nine

Kitchen. Night. Darkness.

In the hallway, we hear HAZEL *and* RICHARD *return from a night out. A sliver of light from the front door enters the room and then goes out again.*

They come towards the kitchen.

RICHARD (*off*)....It's one picture, Hazel.

HAZEL (*off*). I don't want to be in a newspaper, Richard. I'm as big as a house.

RICHARD (*off*). It's a domestic feature. I said we have a great kitchen – real Nigella territory –

They step into the kitchen, he reaches for the light. Can't find it.

– Where the hell's the fucking – Ah /

He finds the dimmer switch, adjusts. Lights on.

ANNIE *is standing by the sink with her back to them. When she speaks she doesn't turn.*

ANNIE. Hi. Sorry. Hi, / I'm – in here.

RICHARD. Oh /

ANNIE. Didn't want to give you a fright.

RICHARD. What are you doing in the dark?

ANNIE *busies herself, keeping her back to them.*

ANNIE. I just had a few things to… clean up. How was the fund-raiser?

HAZEL. Long.

HAZEL *takes off her shoes.*

ANNIE. How was your speech?

HAZEL. A triumph. Standing ovation.

ANNIE. Really?

RICHARD (*bashful*). That's a bit of an – there was a good response to the photographs. Which is why I'm so bloody-minded about taking them. Helps to turn facts and figures into flesh and blood.

HAZEL. They want him to do magazine spreads now and everything. 'At home with *the doctor.*'

RICHARD. Alright, Hazel, you can drop the tone.

ANNIE. So you reached your target?

RICHARD. We reached our – target, yes.

ANNIE *shifts a little, a sense she is avoiding turning around.*

And Hazel's olive oil went down a storm. In the raffle.

HAZEL (*drily*). Yes, that was quite the accomplishment… One less box anyway.

HAZEL *steps in a pile of glass on the floor.*

What happened here?

ANNIE *turns suddenly – her nose and face and the top of her blouse are covered in blood.*

ANNIE. Oh – I meant to clear that / up.

HAZEL. Oh my God. Your face.

RICHARD. Annie /

ANNIE. It's not what you think.

RICHARD. What the hell happened?

ANNIE. Nothing, really. We just had a little – situation. That's all.

HAZEL *looks at the glass on the ground.*

HAZEL. He didn't throw that at you, did he?

ANNIE. Well...

HAZEL. You see, Richard?

RICHARD. Just take it easy for one minute – What happened?

ANNIE *looks a bit dazed.*

ANNIE. I'm not really sure. Really.

RICHARD. Well, where is he?

ANNIE. In bed. But he's grand. He's – fine. You don't need to worry about him.

HAZEL. What have I been saying? How many times have I tried to tell you?

RICHARD. Hazel /

HAZEL. He's getting worse.

ANNIE. I meant to have all this cleaned up before you got in but I think – I think there's something wrong with my lip.

RICHARD. Let me take a look.

RICHARD *sits* ANNIE *down near some lights.*

ANNIE. I didn't want ye coming back to a mess.

RICHARD. Put your head back. Now, what exactly went on?

HAZEL *hands* RICHARD *the first-aid kit. He starts to clean* ANNIE*'s face.*

ANNIE. To be honest I don't – remember. It happened so fast.

HAZEL. It does when he gets like this. It just comes out of nowhere.

ANNIE. He was in a funny mood all evening. Wouldn't look at me, wouldn't eat his dinner, wouldn't play any of our games. And… well I – know I shouldn't have but I got a bit fed up after a while.

HAZEL. Well yes, because he wears you down.

ANNIE. I got a bit angry with him. And I said if he wasn't going to behave himself I'd have to put him to bed. And suddenly he just – got this look on his face and – before I had time to stop him or even realise what he was doing he'd – well, he'd picked up the glass.

RICHARD *stands back.*

RICHARD.…I think we should get you to a hospital.

ANNIE. What? No /

RICHARD. You need a stitch.

ANNIE. Stitches?

RICHARD. Just a couple.

ANNIE. But. Can't you do it?

RICHARD. I'd rather they looked at you there.

HAZEL. It's better to follow protocol.

ANNIE. 'Protocol'?

HAZEL. Do things officially so that if you decided to sue us or something –

RICHARD. What?

ANNIE. I'm not going to sue you.

HAZEL. Well, you don't know that – our son may have damaged your /

RICHARD. Hazel, she's not going to sue us. It's just a cut.

HAZEL. It's important to do things right so that we aren't seen as negligent.

ANNIE. 'Negligent'?

HAZEL. So we didn't put you in danger. As your employers.

RICHARD. Hazel, will you just – There was no danger, Annie. He's a kid.

ANNIE. I'm not suing anyone. I don't even know any lawyers. Except – you.

RICHARD. We're taking you to the hospital because it's the right place to be seen to. It's not a big deal.

HAZEL. But there'll be a record of your visit. Whereas if Richard does it here –

RICHARD looks at HAZEL, *irritated.*

RICHARD. Should one of us go and check on him?

Beat. It's clear from HAZEL's *demeanour that she won't.*

Fine. I'll – do it. (*To* ANNIE.) Be with you in two secs, Annie.

He leaves. ANNIE *holds a tissue against her lip.*

ANNIE. Stitches… It's times like these I wish my mam was here.

HAZEL. Do you want to – call her?

ANNIE. She's dead.

HAZEL. Oh. I didn't – realise.

ANNIE. My da's the one I phone when I phone. But I don't phone much.

HAZEL. No… I'm not – close to my family either. We're very different.

ANNIE. I'd say you were a good lawyer. I couldn't imagine it before, but just then when you were talking about – negligence I could suddenly see you up in court, making a case. A closing – summation or whatever they [call it] – I'd say you were very formidable.

HAZEL. Oh. Well. I wasn't a [barrister] – but yes. I – Yes. That was something I was good at.

ANNIE. Daniel says you won prizes.

HAZEL. Scholarships. Long time ago now. I was a bit of a perfectionist at university. If I thought I wasn't going to ace an exam, I'd just walk out of it. Wouldn't write one word. People thought it was a tactic to get attention. Or – freak the other examinees out, but it wasn't a tactic. I just – couldn't stand the thought of being mediocre. What's the point?

HAZEL *looks around at all the boxes.*

ANNIE....Maybe you'll go back. After the baby.

HAZEL. No, I promised myself I wouldn't.

ANNIE. Why?

HAZEL. That's what I did last time. Cut short my maternity leave.

ANNIE. That must have been stressful.

HAZEL. No. No. It wasn't stressful. It was easy. Work. I liked it. Didn't even mind the late nights... God, when I was at home, I once pushed Daniel's pram up and down the same stretch of road four hundred and seventy-eight times trying to stop him crying. Well – at first to stop him crying but after a while... because there was nothing else to do. Up and down. Up and down. Up. And down. Four hundred and seventy-eight times. I counted. The job was... nothing.

ANNIE. Well, it's a big adjustment. You were used to being so independent and once you have a baby –

HAZEL. You can't go back.

HAZEL *picks up one of the bottles of olive oil.*

Those Sicilians make it seem so... You know, one day I actually watched Alessandra bottle-feed with one hand while rolling dough with the other. She bakes all her own bread too.

ANNIE *dabs at her lip, unsure of what to say.*

HAZEL *puts the oil back.*

…I'm sorry.

ANNIE. For what?

HAZEL. My child. Your – lip.

ANNIE. It's isn't your fault.

HAZEL.…Isn't it?

Beat.

He's always been difficult. He was a difficult birth. But these last few months since I've been at home he's really –

ANNIE. He's just a bit – highly strung, is all.

HAZEL *leans over and takes the tissue from* ANNIE.

HAZEL.…Here… [Let me.]

She begins to wipe ANNIE*'s lip gently.*

I was highly strung. When he was a baby. I was completely – gripped. I had this terrible fear I was going to drop him. I know it sounds crazy but… we had these tiles in the bathroom and in the kitchen and big – concrete steps leading up to the front door and I could just *see* it, you know. Every time I had him in my arms I could just see myself… I was so relieved when other people held him. Isn't that strange? I've heard about women who won't let their babies go but –

ANNIE. Everybody's sensitive with their first.

HAZEL.…Yes. Yes, I suppose.

ANNIE (*pointing to the bump*). It'll be different with this one.

HAZEL. Yes, it will. I know it – will.

ANNIE. You'll know that you know what you're doing.

HAZEL *stops dabbing* ANNIE*'s lip. Looks at her.*

Then –

HAZEL....I left him in a supermarket. On a Saturday
afternoon, last year.

The week before we took that trip to Sicily.

Beat.

Richard doesn't – know.

I'd gotten a phone call, you see. Out of the blue. An
emergency. Managing director of one of our biggest clients
on the line – furious because of some onerous clause he'd
just found on a contract we'd drafted, months before.

I didn't make mistakes on contracts. But they were in the
middle of an employee dispute and things were fraught, so...
He kept ranting and raving about exposure and liability and
incompetence – right there in the supermarket – until finally
all I could do was – plead with him to give me an hour to
just get to the office and go through the paperwork, see what
had gone wrong. And eventually he – agrees. So of course I
abandon the trolley right there in the aisle and rush to the car
and drive like a fury an hour across town.

And – I'm ringing colleagues and gathering the troops because
this client – I mean... And all the time the adrenalin's going
and my mind's racing because I'm thinking about the
company and the consequences and my being up for partner
and what horrors would be unleashed if he does – drop us or
sue us or – God knows what. And I'm determined, *determined*
not to fuck this up. So I park up and grab my briefcase and
rush to the building where some of the others are waiting. And
we're in the lift and I'm doing this big spiel about what we're
going to do and how we're going to salvage this and I'm really
getting on top of it and really psyching myself up to call him
back and fight – when the lift door opens and the little bell
goes and suddenly I remember – Daniel.

I've left Daniel back at the supermarket.

Just – completely forgot he'd been with me.

ANNIE *stares at her.*

...Course I went straight back. And he was fine. Someone
had found him and he was – fine.

ANNIE. Thank God.

HAZEL. Yes.

ANNIE. Imagine.

HAZEL. I do. I do – imagine. All the time… What if he'd…
What if someone had… What would I have done?… What
would I have said?… How could I possibly have explained I
just – forgot him because something came up at the office
and for one brief moment I felt like myself.

Beat.

So, no. I won't – go back.

Beat.

I'm glad though that you've seen.

ANNIE. Seen?

HAZEL. What he can be capable of. That he needs to be reined
in. I know that look he gets.

ANNIE. 'Look'?

HAZEL. Like he knows exactly what he's doing. Like he's
deliberately trying to – punish.

ANNIE. What are you talking about?

HAZEL.… You said he got a look before he picked up the /
glass.

ANNIE. No. I didn't.

HAZEL. Yes, you – did.

ANNIE. No I didn't. He's a child. He was just being bold. It's
what children do. And sure who could blame him after what
you've just… You're the one who should be ashamed of
yourself.

HAZEL *smarts.*

RICHARD *comes back in.*

RICHARD. Right, he's asleep. Like butter wouldn't melt. I –
Well, look, we'll decide how to deal with this tomorrow.
Annie, I think we should get on.

ANNIE *gets up quickly, looking at* HAZEL *somewhat warily.*

ANNIE. Sure. Yeah. I'm – ready.

RICHARD *glances out the window.*

RICHARD. Are they having another party next door?

HAZEL. Do they ever seem to stop?

HAZEL *takes out a dustpan and brush, begins to sweep up the broken glass.*

RICHARD. Lucky for some… We'll try not to be too late.

HAZEL (*not looking*). Fine.

RICHARD *hangs back a second longer.*

RICHARD.…Have another think about that article, will you?

HAZEL. I've thought about it, Richard. I've made it very clear.

RICHARD. It's just one picture.

HAZEL. Well, I don't want to do it.

RICHARD. It's good coverage. It'd really help with –

HAZEL. For God's sake, I've just told you – don't you hear one word I say? I don't want to do it. I am not up to it, alright? I am not up to playing your goddamn trophy fucking wife.

Silence.

RICHARD.…Fine. That's… Yeah. Fine. Thanks for the support.

RICHARD *and* ANNIE *go,* RICHARD *placing a hand on* ANNIE*'s back as they do.*

HAZEL *turns suddenly, wanting to say something softer – Sorry? – but doesn't.*

The tinkling music from next door can be heard faintly through the window. HAZEL *stands somewhat shakily and looks at the broken glass in the dustpan.*

She crosses the room and drops it into the bin.

Ten

Later that night.

The room is in darkness. DANIEL *comes in in his pyjamas.*

He looks around, then up at the cupboard where HAZEL *put the camera.*

He pulls out a chair and brings it towards the cupboard.

He stands up on it trying to reach.

Light from the hallway creeps into the room. The front door opens. Sounds heard.

DANIEL *jumps off the chair and crawls under the table to hide.* RICHARD *comes towards the door, switching on the light.*

RICHARD. What's the point of having friends in high places if you have to sit in A & E for two bloody hours? Ooh, too bright –

He adjusts the light. ANNIE *enters behind him, a small plaster on her lip.*

ANNIE. And I didn't even need the stitches.

RICHARD. Glue's the same thing, young lady. Don't you dare start questioning my expertise.

She smiles at him.

ANNIE. Course not.

He opens the fridge and takes out a bottle of white wine.

RICHARD. Think we both deserve a drink after that marathon, don't you?

ANNIE *gets two glasses. He pours.*

So go on then. Finish your story.

ANNIE. Which story?

RICHARD. The one about you and that little friend of yours
sneaking into the cemetery at midnight to sit by Yeats's grave.

ANNIE. I did – finish it.

RICHARD. Oh. That was the punchline? That you just sat there
all night by his grave?

ANNIE. It's not a very good story, I suppose.

RICHARD. No, it is, it is. The way you tell it. With your –
accent, it's very poetic.

ANNIE. It's not poetic.

RICHARD. It is.

ANNIE. It's just my accent.

RICHARD. There are no dead poets where I'm from, I assure
you. To me, you are the essence of exotic, Annie.

He gives her a glass. They move towards the table.

Underneath it, DANIEL *shifts quietly, careful not to be seen.*

ANNIE. My mam's buried not far from there. In the new
cemetery. Yeats is in the old part, so can't exactly say she's
buried with William Butler Yeats but… not far.

RICHARD *raises his glass.*

RICHARD. To your mother.

ANNIE *clinks her glass against his.*

ANNIE. Mam.

She drinks.

…She drowned. When I was nine.

RICHARD. Oh. How awful.

ANNIE. Did it to herself, they reckon. That's what's awful. She
said she was going to get some milk. She told me and my
sister. She put on her coat and her brown hat and some
lipstick and she said, 'I'm going to get some milk. Keep an
eye on the others.' And she made a sort of face in the mirror

at herself. Don't know what it was meant to mean, that face. But anyway, she went. And it took them a week to find her. We never got to see her after that on account of – what she must've looked like after the week in the water. So… I always think of her in front of the mirror instead…

She takes a sip of her drink. RICHARD *shakes his head.*

RICHARD. Fuck.

ANNIE. Yeah.

RICHARD. Annie.

She takes another drink.

You're a wonder.

ANNIE. I'm not a wonder.

RICHARD. Yes, you are.

He takes her hands in his.

ANNIE. Sad things happen to people.

RICHARD. Yes, they do. Yes they fucking do. Sad things happen to people. Let's drink to that.

They clink glasses. Drink. She looks at him.

ANNIE. Has anything… sad happened to you?

He thinks.

RICHARD. You know, I think I'm one of the lucky ones. Which is why I'm so in awe of people like you. Real people.

She smiles.

ANNIE. I often wonder about what she was thinking. When she did it. What must have been going through her head – as she climbed up onto that bridge at seven o'clock in the evening.

RICHARD. Well, who could possibly say.

ANNIE. It was November. The water would have been ice. That's what probably killed her in the end… She used sing. A lot. Do – disturbed people sing?

RICHARD. Some. I imagine.

ANNIE. She sang. All the time.

From under the table, DANIEL *leans closer.*

She could've told someone. She should've. She had a duty.
There were six of us – needing and depending and loving her.
She owed us more than just to fling herself off a bridge so's
everyone in the whole county knew we weren't enough to
keep her going. For years afterwards we used fight over her
nightdress. Cos that was the only thing that still had her smell.

Beat.

You were right to have hired me.

RICHARD. I know that.

ANNIE. You were right to want to keep an eye. It was the right
thing to do.

RICHARD. Yes.

RICHARD *stares at* ANNIE.

God, what you've been through, Annie. I had no idea...
When you sent through your pictures I thought – Well, I just
thought, what a lovely girl. What great experience she's had
but it wasn't –

ANNIE. You didn't think I was pretty?

RICHARD. Yes. No, of course. Yes. I just didn't think you were
– tragic.

Beat.

Sorry. I meant that as a compliment.

She smiles and takes a drink.

ANNIE. Can I tell you something?

RICHARD. Please.

ANNIE. ...I knew who you were before I came here.

Beat.

I read about you a few years back. In a magazine. You were working out in – Peshawar, I think. And there was a big picture of you in a green jacket in the middle of a group of children. You were talking about the sort of injuries you were treating there – ones caused by car bombs or home-made bombs with bits of metal or nails or… And you were talking about the kids, how they didn't have access to the treatments they needed. And you – wanted to change that. You wanted to be able to offer a crack team of really well-trained experts from all over – plastic surgeons and doctors, the best in their fields – who could give their time and their expertise for a week or a weekend /

RICHARD. Yes /

ANNIE. And help. You said it was your mission.

RICHARD. It is. It still is.

ANNIE. You made such an impression. I remember reading it and thinking – that man is a great man, *that* man… I tore it out and everything. Isn't that stupid?

RICHARD. Well, I have to tell you, Annie, the first time I ever went out – to Afghanistan, I wasn't such a great man. Wanted to come home, truth be told. They had us doing nine, ten operations a day, barbaric conditions, barely enough anaesthetic to keep the patients from sitting up mid-op with their wounds still open. I'd never seen anything like it. The chaos. The sheer. I remember thinking – what in God's name am I doing here? What has any of this got to do with me? I sew a man up today, tomorrow for all I know he could be – planting a roadside bomb. Where does this end this – cycle of… But then I thought about it. And I realised. I can save a life. And if I can save a life, I can change a life. It's got everything to do with me. It's got everything to do with all of us. We have to look after each other.

ANNIE. When the agency sent through your picture and I recognised you – it was like fate. It was like – life was handing me a chance and if I didn't seize it…

RICHARD. Hazel used to say things like that. When I first met her.

ANNIE. At school.

RICHARD. University. She was – friends with a girl in my house. But she wasn't like any of the girls in my house. The daughters of barristers and surgeons. Hazel's family ran a corner shop. She was the first one to go to university. She'd such – grit. Back then, Hazel. Such steel. She could do anything she put her mind to.

He thinks about this, then looks at ANNIE.

Don't ever change, Annie. When you grow up. Don't ever lose this [quality]… It's precious.

Beat.

ANNIE.…Could I – show you something?

RICHARD. Of course.

Under the table, DANIEL *strains to see what she is doing.*

ANNIE. It's kind of… Well, it's kind of personal.

She gestures to her blouse.

I have to take this off.

RICHARD. Oh.

ANNIE. Would that be strange? It's just… I'd like to have your opinion on something. Medically.

RICHARD. Well, I am a – doctor. I suppose.

ANNIE. You've seen it all before.

RICHARD. Yes.

He takes a drink. She stands up and starts to unbutton her blouse. He watches.

It takes however long it needs to take. Before she opens her blouse she hesitates, looking him directly in the eye.

ANNIE. Promise me you won't tell anyone?

RICHARD *looks at her, nods.* ANNIE *opens her blouse.*

There is a huge red zig-zag scar at the front of her body.

RICHARD. Bloody hell, where did that come from?

ANNIE. I've had it for years… My da –

RICHARD. Your father? Your father did this to you? What sort of animal /

ANNIE. Don't – No, that's not why I'm. I don't want to blame him.

RICHARD. You don't want to blame him – Annie, look at you.

ANNIE. There were six of us. He couldn't manage – he was mad with grief – he wasn't in his right mind.

RICHARD. So what he just –

ANNIE. It was only the once.

    RICHARD *looks closely at the scar.*

RICHARD. What was it? A belt?

ANNIE. He was drunk – he lashed so hard the buckle got stuck in my skin and when he pulled /

RICHARD. Damnit, Annie. The man is a monster.

ANNIE. He was so sorry after. You should've seen him.

    He touches her, runs his hands over the mark.

    I just want to know if you can get it off.

    Beat.

    Can you – get it off? You've worked with worse. I mean, it's not an acid burn, it's not a bomb. It's just a – Surely some grafts or – or a lift or – I just. It's just – Every time I look at myself – it's there and it's so ugly and it's so – unnecessary and I just want it to be gone because it makes me think – it makes me think of hate when I look at it. It makes me think of the worst that humans can be. It makes me just want to take a scissors and – so… I want to know if something can be done. Can you – do something for me? Do you think? Can you help me in some – I just don't want have to look in the mirror every day for the rest of my life and see… this.

    Silence. RICHARD *stares at her.*

Then slowly he runs his hand up over her stomach, over her neck, up to her face.

RICHARD. Why would anybody ever want to hurt you, Annie? You're the gentlest creature in the world.

ANNIE. It's just so ugly.

RICHARD. You're not ugly, Annie.

ANNIE. I'm not beautiful.

Beat.

Hazel's... beautiful. Isn't she?

RICHARD. She – is.

ANNIE. I'm not like her, am I?

RICHARD....No. No, you're – different.

ANNIE. Do you think I ever could be... like Hazel? You know. Living in a house like this, with a child and a shiny kitchen and a brilliant husband... Or do you think people like me who come from shit and have shit happen them, have to stay in the shit from which they grew for the rest of their lives, cos that's what they know and that's what they deserve and that's what's carved out on their bodies and no one can ever get it off?

Beat.

Do you think I'll always have to be the nanny in a place like this?

RICHARD. No.

ANNIE. No?

RICHARD. No, I don't. I really... don't.

She comes a little closer to him, takes his hand. He looks at the scars.

I could get this off. If you wanted. I could. And I will. If that's what you – want... I'm not sure it's what I'd want, though.

Beat.

Because I think – I think you, standing like that. Like this.
Now. As you are – scars and marks and... I think you are one
of the most beautiful things I have ever seen in my whole
life, Annie. And I'm not sure I'd want to take that away.
From you. From me. From anyone. I'm not sure it's mine to
take away.

*He runs his hands gently over her face, careful of her plaster
– and kisses her. They start to undress.*

*From underneath, DANIEL strains to see as RICHARD lifts
ANNIE onto the table.*

Eleven

A sense of time passing.

*A 'How to Learn Italian' audio plays on a CD player or iPod –
a voice repeating stock phrases in English and Italian.*

HAZEL *and* ANNIE *are in the kitchen stepping around one
another, tense, not making eye contact.* HAZEL *is trying to
listen to the Italian while tidying boxes.*

DANIEL *is doing his homework at the table.*

ANNIE *puts a plate of sandwiches in front of him.*

HAZEL *rewinds the audio, so the last few phrases are repeated.*

DANIEL *pushes the sandwiches away.*

ANNIE *pushes the sandwiches towards him.*

HAZEL *rewinds the audio with growing frustration at trying to
retain the Italian.*

DANIEL *pushes the sandwiches away.*

*The audio gets stuck and starts to repeat the same word over
and over.* HAZEL *tries to turn it off.*

ANNIE *pushes the sandwiches towards* DANIEL *once more.*

HAZEL *bangs the iPod or stereo.*

The audio stops suddenly.

DANIEL *pushes the sandwiches away with force. They fall on the floor.*

HAZEL *looks over at* ANNIE *and* DANIEL.

ANNIE *kneels down and starts to pick the sandwiches up.*

Twelve

HAZEL *holds the phone to her ear with one hand and a letter with the other.*

HAZEL (*re: the letter*). I don't understand. I thought we'd fixed this. (*To* DANIEL.) I thought I'd made it very clear.

RICHARD. We're going to sort it out.

HAZEL (*into the phone*). Hello? *Ciao?* – Hello?

RICHARD. Look, you're busy. Myself and Annie will go –

She hangs up.

HAZEL. No, hang on.

RICHARD (*to* ANNIE). I think we should keep this as simple as possible.

HAZEL *looks at the letter.*

HAZEL. They say they want to meet with the parents.

RICHARD. And I'm one of the parents.

HAZEL. But she's not.

RICHARD. I thought you were working this afternoon. Speaking to /

HAZEL. Yes but /

RICHARD. So you do that and we'll do this.

HAZEL. But /

RICHARD. Look, I'd rather be over in surgery myself, quite frankly, but when Annie called –

HAZEL. Annie – called? You called – him?

RICHARD. Yes.

HAZEL. Why?

RICHARD. Hazel.

HAZEL. I've been here all morning. You never said one word to me.

ANNIE. Well, I made a decision.

HAZEL. …Sorry?

ANNIE. I thought – given the seriousness it would be better if /

RICHARD. We don't have time for this. I've to be back in two hours. Let's just get it sorted. Annie, get your coat.

HAZEL *looks at the letter.*

HAZEL. They're talking about 'repeated incidents'.

RICHARD. I know.

HAZEL (*to* ANNIE). What do they mean by 'repeated incidents'? Why is this the first I've heard about it?

RICHARD. Annie didn't want to worry you.

HAZEL. Annie didn't want to – worry me?

ANNIE. You seemed a bit overwhelmed the last time.

HAZEL. What?

RICHARD. You let that headmistress bully you.

HAZEL. No I didn't.

ANNIE. Well, she certainly upset you. And I just didn't see the point of getting you all – worked up again.

HAZEL. Excuse me?

ANNIE. When Richard could just as easily handle it.

HAZEL *stares at her, trying to process.*

RICHARD. There's a simple explanation, Hazel. We just need to speak to the little girl's parents.

HAZEL. No. No. This is nonsense. We shouldn't have to speak to her parents – we shouldn't have to – be doing anything.

HAZEL *turns to* DANIEL.

I thought we agreed you were to leave that little girl alone.

DANIEL *doesn't say anything.*

I thought we agreed you were going to behave.

DANIEL. I didn't /

ANNIE. There's more to it than that /

HAZEL *rounds on* DANIEL. *Perhaps pulls at him.*

HAZEL. Do you think this is funny or something? Making me look stupid. Making me look like I can't control my own child.

ANNIE. Hey. Don't /

HAZEL. I told you to stop messing with that little girl /

RICHARD. Hazel, calm down.

HAZEL. I will not calm down. I can't take any more. This has got to stop, Daniel. Do you hear me? /

RICHARD *intervenes.*

RICHARD. Hazel /

HAZEL. THIS HAS GOT TO STOP.

DANIEL (*suddenly*). She has marks on her face.

HAZEL.…What? What are you saying?

DANIEL. Mia.

RICHARD. The little girl – the little Chinese girl had a – birthmark, it transpires.

HAZEL. A – birthmark?

ANNIE. It's why she's so sensitive. The headmistress didn't mention it the last time cos –

RICHARD. They got it fixed, by a doctor.

DANIEL. It's still there.

RICHARD. Yes, it's – There's a little scar or something. He's completely fascinated by it. It's cos of all the stuff he knows that I do and we think – I think – that if we just go in there and explain –

DANIEL. She went to a bad doctor.

RICHARD. Daniel.

DANIEL. She did.

RICHARD. Well, that really isn't for us to – say. (*To* HAZEL.) I think they just need to understand where it's coming from. That he isn't trying to –

DANIEL. When you fix Annie's mark you won't still see it.

RICHARD *looks at* DANIEL.

RICHARD. Pardon?

DANIEL. When you fix Annie's mark, it'll be gone. Won't it?

HAZEL.…What mark? Annie doesn't have any marks.

DANIEL. Yes she does.

RICHARD. Come on, we should go /

DANIEL. Under her jumper.

ANNIE. Daniel. What are you – saying?

HAZEL. Under her – jumper? What are you talking about?

DANIEL (*pointing to* RICHARD). He looked at them.

ANNIE. What?

DANIEL. When he lifted her onto the table. He kissed them.

ANNIE *looks a little desperately at* RICHARD.

RICHARD. Daniel, mate, what the hell are you on about?

DANIEL. I saw you.

RICHARD. You saw me what?

HAZEL *stares at* RICHARD.

DANIEL. In the middle of the night. I saw you kiss the marks on Annie.

DANIEL *seems nervous, a sense he knows he has transgressed.*

ANNIE. I don't have any – marks on me, Daniel.

DANIEL. Yes you do. All here. You showed them to him.

RICHARD *looks at* ANNIE, *then at* HAZEL, *then starts laughing.*

RICHARD. This is – I don't – I have absolutely no idea where he's getting this. Daniel, mate, I have no idea what sort of TV you've been watching lately, but that's really –

HAZEL *walks across the room and stands in front of* ANNIE.

What are you doing?

HAZEL. Lift up your blouse, please.

ANNIE. What? No.

HAZEL. …I'd like you to lift up your blouse and let me see.

RICHARD. Hazel, don't be outrageous.

HAZEL. I want to know what's under there.

RICHARD. There's nothing – under there, for God's sake.

HAZEL. I want to know if he's telling the truth.

RICHARD. Of course he isn't.

HAZEL. Where would he have gotten the idea that you have marks on your chest?

ANNIE. I don't know. Daniel…

RICHARD. He could have gotten it anywhere, Hazel. God, you've said it yourself a million times. Children make things up.

HAZEL. Then lift up your blouse and prove it.

RICHARD. Come on, Hazel. Stop it.

HAZEL. Unless you have something to hide. Have you something to hide, Annie?

ANNIE. No, of course not. I don't – have any marks.

RICHARD. Hazel, she doesn't have to answer to you. How dare you just walk over there and make insane –

HAZEL. If there's nothing to hide it doesn't matter. Please.

Beat.

Lift up your blouse.

ANNIE *doesn't move.*

A stalemate as the women look at each other.

Suddenly HAZEL *lunges at* ANNIE *and starts to pull up her shirt.* ANNIE *fights her off.*

ANNIE. What are you – Jesus /

HAZEL. I want to see

ANNIE. You can't just /

HAZEL. Let me see /

ANNIE. Stop it /

HAZEL. I want to know.

ANNIE. Richard /

HAZEL. What's under there, Annie?

HAZEL *backs* ANNIE *up to the wall, starts pulling at her wildly.*

ANNIE. Leave me alone – Richard /

HAZEL. What have you got to hide?

ANNIE. Richard, please. She's hurting me.

HAZEL. I saw something.

RICHARD *pulls* HAZEL *off* ANNIE.

RICHARD. Hazel, for fuck's sake, get a grip on yourself /

HAZEL. There was a mark. I saw /

RICHARD. What the hell do you think you're doing? /

HAZEL. I saw a mark. I SAW A MARK /

RICHARD. Talk about fucking lawsuits.

HAZEL (*to* ANNIE). *You're lying.*

RICHARD. He's lying. *He* is lying. God, Hazel, you can't just go attacking people like that.

HAZEL. I saw something.

RICHARD. You're deranged. Annie – God. I'm sorry I'm... are you alright?

ANNIE *nods.*

She smoothes her top down, trying to regain her composure.

This is... That is – completely unacceptable, Hazel. Daniel, look what you've started. Do you see how dangerous it is to make up stories?

DANIEL *doesn't say anything.*

What did I tell you about lying, hmmn? Liars are dangerous people. Most of the bloody problems in the world today are caused by – You do not want to be a liar... Now tell Hazel you made it up.

DANIEL *doesn't say anything.*

Tell her, Daniel.

HAZEL. Why would he make that up?

RICHARD. Because.

HAZEL. Because what?

ANNIE. Because he wanted to punish you.

HAZEL *looks at* ANNIE.

You're the one who says he has a streak in him. You're the one who says he gets a look. Well, maybe you're [right] – I mean, I couldn't see it before but –

ANNIE *looks at* RICHARD *for help*.

– if he's willing to stand there and say a thing like that and
not feel the slightest ounce of… maybe you're right. Maybe
there is something – wrong with him.

RICHARD. Daniel, mate, your behaviour lately has been pretty
troubling. And you know I'm very fair and I don't like to
come down hard, but this – can't keep happening. If this
keeps happening we're going to have to think of some
serious – We're going to have to sort you out.

ANNIE. You shouldn't make up stories, Daniel.

RICHARD. Now I'm going to give you another chance to tell
the truth here. So that Hazel doesn't spend her whole night
worrying. Tell her you made it up. The thing about Annie's
marks and me – doing whatever. Tell Hazel it was a lie.

Silence.

Daniel.

DANIEL *doesn't say anything*.

Alright, that's it. Go to your room.

DANIEL *doesn't move*.

I will not have a liar in my kitchen. Go.

DANIEL *doesn't move*.

Get out of my sight, Daniel. Now.

He pulls DANIEL *off the chair*.

I don't want to look at you – if you're going to make up
stories. I don't want to see your face. Get out. Get out. JUST
GET OUT. NOW.

RICHARD *pushes* DANIEL *out the door*. ANNIE *takes a
step towards him as though about to intervene, but sees*
HAZEL *watching and stops*.

The three of them stand in the room.

Silence.

(*To* HAZEL.) I think you owe Annie an apology.

Silence.

Hazel. I think you should say sorry to Annie.

ANNIE. No, it's okay. I don't. It's okay. He's just going through a phase, that's all. He's… It's since we took away the spider. Ever since we took away the spider he's been acting out.

RICHARD. God. Yes. You're [right] – The damn – spider. Of course.

HAZEL.…Of course what?

RICHARD. Well, of course that's what this is. The fucking [spider] – Why did you ever buy the bloody thing, Hazel? It's been nothing but trouble.

HAZEL. This has nothing to do with the spider.

ANNIE. Well, no, I think it – does actually. Cos – when we took it away, if you remember that's when he really started – misbehaving.

RICHARD. You're right. Yes. You're absolutely. Jesus. You don't give a kid something and then take it away. Of course that's going to mess with his head. It's obvious. No wonder he's throwing things and concocting – stories. He's confused. We've confused him.

HAZEL. This is not about a bloody spider.

RICHARD. Maybe it's about time you started taking some responsibility.

HAZEL. Me?

RICHARD. Yes, you. You were the one encouraging him to keep secrets. Buying him – pets. Behaving in a totally inappropriate –

RICHARD *trips over one of the boxes of olive oil and kicks it.*

Fuck! Is there one room in this goddamn house that isn't full of boxes of olive oil?

HAZEL. I was just calling them when you came in.

RICHARD. Well, call them. Bloody call them. I thought you were supposed to sell them, Hazel. I thought that that was the point.

ANNIE. I'll go and get my – jacket.

RICHARD. Yes, do that. Let's sort this mess out once and for all.

ANNIE *goes out*.

RICHARD *takes a breath and goes to the sideboard to search for his keys*.

HAZEL *watches him*.

HAZEL. ...I saw something, Richard. I saw a mark.

Beat.

He wasn't lying.

RICHARD. *Yes*, he was.

HAZEL. No, he wasn't. He – wasn't.

RICHARD. Jesus Christ. Isn't this what you've been angling for? You're the one who been trying to convince us he's the devil.

HAZEL. ...What?... No. That's... I wasn't... I was just –

RICHARD (*exasperated*). Look, you have got to get yourself in order. Alright? I've done everything I can but at the end of the day – you are going to have to do something about this. About yourself. Cos honestly – honestly, Hazel, I'm not sure how much more I can take.

He walks out.

Silence.

HAZEL *looks at the phone. She presses redial and very slowly puts it to her ear*.

HAZEL. Hello? *Ciao?... Lei parla inglese?...* Is Alessandra there? I'd like to speak with –

DANIEL *comes to the door, watches her.*

Posso parlare con Allesandra – there's been a mistake with my – *posso parlare* – *posso* – I've been emailing – please, I don't know how to – please – I don't – I can't – please…

She hangs up the phone.

With a cry she flings it across the room.

She turns suddenly to see DANIEL *standing in the doorway.*

They look at one another.

Thirteen

RICHARD *and* HAZEL *alone in the kitchen.*

Night. Very late. Maybe the early hours of the morning.

RICHARD *is dressed, and a very economically packed suitcase sits on the floor. In front of* HAZEL *on the table is a small box of pills.*

HAZEL. I don't want you to go.

RICHARD. Hazel /

HAZEL. I'm asking you not to go.

RICHARD. The car is on its way.

HAZEL. Please.

RICHARD. It's three days. This is a once-in-a-lifetime opportunity. To have a film crew willing to come with us– to show the work we're doing first-hand –

HAZEL. It's not safe.

He sighs.

RICHARD. Just take the pills.

HAZEL. I don't want to take the pills.

RICHARD. You agreed.

HAZEL. Why do I need to take pills?

RICHARD. Because that's what people do when they're like this. This is perfectly manageable, Hazel, if you just take it in hand.

HAZEL. Something's going to happen.

RICHARD. No it's not.

HAZEL (*re: the bump*). It could happen any time. You don't know.

RICHARD. Nothing is going to –

HAZEL. I'm not ready.

RICHARD. You have a whole month to go. Why do you think I'm packing all these trips in now? I'm packing them in now so that I'll be here like I said I would. I'll do my best not to be late.

HAZEL. I don't have the choice of being late. I *have* to be here.

RICHARD. I want to know that you are going to be reasonable while I'm away. I want to know that you are going to cooperate –

HAZEL. 'Cooperate'?

RICHARD. With Annie.

HAZEL.…Is Annie the boss now?

RICHARD. No. I just –

HAZEL. Did you fuck her?

RICHARD. Hazel, please /

HAZEL. You can tell me. There's no one around. It's only us.

RICHARD. Are you ever going to stop this?

HAZEL. We're both adults, Richard. We're both old enough to know the way it works. I can see how she looks at you. I can understand what that must – do for you. At a time like this when your wife's so clearly... Just please let's stop scrabbling around on our hands and knees pretending what's happening isn't happening. Because I can't take that any more – I'm losing my... I don't care if you did – I just need you to tell me – I just need you to – tell me. Let's just please just – tell the honest truth.

RICHARD. The truth?

HAZEL. Yes.

RICHARD. The truth will make you feel better?

HAZEL. I believe so, yes.

RICHARD. Did I fuck her?

HAZEL. Yes.

He looks at her.

She waits.

Something on the tip of his tongue.

RICHARD....No, Hazel. No. I didn't – fuck her, as I have told you a million times. Can't you see how irrational this is?

HAZEL. How?

RICHARD. Because, God, she's – from Sligo. She's not exactly some bit of totty wandering around the house in a pair of hot pants. She's just – she's just a poor bloody farm girl whose mother died when she was young and who's exorcising her demons looking after other people's kids. Doing a better job for them than was done for her. She's a pure soul, Hazel. Life dealt her some crappy blows and she's making the best of them. That you could be threatened by that. For God's sake, someone like you to someone like her...

HAZEL. What?

RICHARD. Nothing.

HAZEL. What?

RICHARD. You just don't know how good you have it.

HAZEL. Sorry?

RICHARD. There are women your age who would kill for what you've got.

Beat.

The woman I married was not interested in sitting around feeling sorry for herself because she felt a bit down every now and then. The woman I married was courageous and ambitious and cared about things outside of these four walls.

HAZEL. I care about things. I paid for these four walls. I helped you pay for them. I supported you when you started volunteering –

RICHARD. And what am I doing now? Olive oil is not going to pay the mortgage, Hazel. This is a hobby. A distraction. Something so you don't get bored changing nappies in the afternoon. Isn't it? I mean, I thought we both got that. I thought that's what you wanted.

HAZEL. That isn't what I wanted.

RICHARD. What did you want?

HAZEL. I wanted – to be good. I wanted it to feel good. I thought if I just stayed here, if I just stayed home –

RICHARD. You wanted to give up being a lawyer, I supported your decision. You wanted to work from home, I supported that decision too. I have done every fucking thing I can possibly do to accommodate you and you still resent me. There is nothing more I can do, Hazel. I can't win. Just don't piss all over the one bloody thing that gives meaning to my life, which is working in places where people are too poor to be depressed. Or too ravaged by the elements or the bombs which have killed their families and flattened their houses to realise how fucking fucked they really are. Do not deprive me of making a difference to their lives – because *clearly* I don't make one ounce of difference to yours.

Silence. She looks at him.

HAZEL. Before Annie ever got here, I sent you a message.

RICHARD. I do the work I do for a reason. I have given up a lot /

HAZEL. You were in Haiti and I couldn't – get hold of you by phone /

RICHARD. You know, I could sit in my office injecting botulism into women's foreheads week in week out if I chose to. I could put away a tidy sum and call myself a respected member of society at that game. Plenty do. But that would make me want to throw myself under a train, quite frankly. I have other things to offer. I want to make the world a fairer place.

HAZEL. Did you ever get my message?

RICHARD. Hazel.

HAZEL. I'm asking you did you ever get the message that I sent?

RICHARD. Have you listened to a bloody – Yes, I got it.

HAZEL. And what did it say?

RICHARD. I had no choice, I had to stay.

HAZEL. Just tell me what it said.

RICHARD. You can't keep /

HAZEL. What did it say?

RICHARD. It said – 'Help.' It said 'Please help me. I'm frightened. I don't think I can do this by myself.' I read what it said and I did.

HAZEL. What did you do?

RICHARD. I helped you. The only way I could from the other side of the world. I hired Annie. To help you. I have nothing to feel guilty about here, Hazel. I did everything in my power. And you know it.

He stands up and moves to the sink, frustrated.

There are things I need to do.

HAZEL. There are things I'd like to do too.

RICHARD. Then go and do them. Nothing's stopping you.

She points to her huge swollen stomach.

HAZEL. *This* is stopping me. This – is a prison. I'm trapped.

RICHARD. Well, you brought it on yourself. You wanted this baby.

HAZEL. I wanted to get it right.

RICHARD. Jesus, you're not the only woman to have ever given birth. Women have babies all the time. Brilliant women politicians and lawyers and fucking – Sky News war correspondents have babies and go back to work. No one told you to sell out.

Beat.

You know, that's the thing about this whole generation. You are so goddamn entitled. You want it every way. You want to be the big high-powered career-women with the salary to boot and you want to be the earth mothers at home drinking goat's milk and breast-feeding and growing your own goddamn vegetables. But you're not willing to sacrifice anything to do it. You're not willing to say if I want to have this, I have to give up that. If I choose to do this, I can't do that. You see sacrifice as the curse of your sex alone. As if men don't give things up all the time. Every day, every fucking hour… And then when you've got it all, when you've engineered your life to be exactly as you want it to be, you're still fucking miserable because you had to hire a nanny.

HAZEL. You hired her.

RICHARD. It's three days.

HAZEL. You say that every time.

RICHARD. No I don't /

HAZEL. And the last trip was supposed to be the last trip, but here you are again with your bags packed. How can I believe a word you say?

RICHARD. It's three fucking days, Hazel. And then I'm back here. With you. And Daniel. Removing moles and injecting botox and doing all the things you want me to be doing. I'll be doing them right here.

She stares at him, some sort of realisation dawning.

HAZEL....Wanting to throw yourself under a train.

RICHARD. Hazel.

She stares him, then down at her bump.

HAZEL. We're monsters. You and I. We're... monsters. We've made such a mess.

RICHARD*'s phone beeps.*

RICHARD....That's the car.

HAZEL. Don't go.

RICHARD. I have to go.

RICHARD *puts on his jacket.*

HAZEL. We have to fix this. We did this together. We have to set it right. Richard /

He picks up his bag, then leans in to give her a kiss.

RICHARD. I'll see you at the weekend.

She holds onto him.

HAZEL. Please, Richard. We can't keep papering the cracks. We can't keep lying.

Beat.

I'm a terrible person.

She puts her hand on her bump.

I've made a terrible mistake.

He kisses her cheek. Then pushes her away.

RICHARD....Take the pills.

Black.

Fourteen

Kitchen. The next morning.

Some of the boxes and bottles of oil may have been moved or tidied.

ANNIE *is in the doorway, her anorak on, a shopping bag in each hand.*

Her suitcase is on the floor, open, bits of clothing hanging out of it – clearly packed in a hurry.

HAZEL *is standing beside it, quite still. She looks exhausted and it's clear she hasn't slept.*

ANNIE *looks from the suitcase, to* HAZEL, *then back to the suitcase again.*

Then she steps past them into the kitchen and begins to unpack the shopping as though nothing is happening.

HAZEL *watches.*

Beat.

ANNIE (*calmly*)....There's been a misunderstanding.

   Beat.

   There's been some sort of – misunderstanding. I just took
   him to school. I just dropped him at the school and got the
   shopping and came back here. I just did what I always do.
   Every day. Nothing different.

   ANNIE *turns to put something into the cupboard, glancing
   briefly at the suitcase.*

   HAZEL *doesn't move.*

   ANNIE *keeps putting things away – trying to carry on as
   normal.*

There was a queue this morning. And a late delivery. But I got most of it. I got most of what you had – on the list. And I can go back later. If there's something important. If there's something else that you – need. So...

ANNIE *glances at* HAZEL, *a little unsure then carries on.*

HAZEL *points to one of the bottles of olive oil.*

HAZEL (*quietly*). Do you want to take one of those?

ANNIE....Sorry?

HAZEL. The oil. Do you want to take a bottle with you? You can, I don't mind... I'm sending them back tomorrow. Every last one.

ANNIE *stops, looks at* HAZEL, *beginning to process.*

ANNIE. You're... sending them back?

HAZEL *nods.*

HAZEL. Finally got through to Alessandra.

HAZEL *turns and moves slowly to the sideboard.*

She picks up a knife and methodically starts to cut some bread.

I tried to tell her we were drowning in the stuff. And I tried to tell her I hadn't half enough stockists. And I tried to tell her that it turns out I don't actually know the first fucking thing about olive oil – selling it or otherwise – because I'm not like her. I'll never be – like her. I don't seem to have the skill... But I'm not sure she understood. With the language – barrier.

Beat.

HAZEL *gestures to the oil again.*

Go on, take one. Put it in your bag.

Beat.

ANNIE *looks around.*

ANNIE....Does Richard know about this? What you're... Cos I think I should speak to him. I'm supposed to tell him. I'm supposed to let him know what's going on.

ANNIE *takes a step towards* HAZEL, *reaches for the phone.*

HAZEL *covers it with her hand.*

He hired me. There's a contract. You can't just turn around and –

ANNIE *reaches for the phone more forcefully.* HAZEL *lets her have it.*

He has a right to know what's going on.

ANNIE *dials a number quickly.*

HAZEL *goes back to making the sandwich.*

ANNIE *paces – it's clearly going to answering machine.*

HAZEL. It's a theme of his. Not answering. At life's crucial junctures.

ANNIE *tries again. A hint of desperation.*

He's probably out with that woman. That journalist. The one who said he was so very photogenic.

ANNIE *hangs up quickly and turns on* HAZEL.

ANNIE. Richard left me in charge. Okay? He told me. He said – I'm to be in charge.

HAZEL *looks at her, takes this in.*

HAZEL.…Do you want to check your room?

HAZEL *takes out something to wrap the sandwiches.*

ANNIE. I'm not doing anything until I've spoken to him.

HAZEL. I doubt I missed much but you might want to make sure.

ANNIE. I promised.

HAZEL. Yes… Yes, I have a very good idea of what you promised, Annie, and I no longer want you in my house.

Beat.

HAZEL *picks up the sandwich.*

I'll put these in your bag.

ANNIE. This is ridiculous. I haven't done anything. Leave my things alone.

HAZEL *ignores her and crosses the room.*

HAZEL. Your services aren't required any longer.

ANNIE. Don't touch that, do you hear me?

HAZEL. It's time that you went home.

ANNIE. I said don't touch it. Leave it, please.

HAZEL *reaches down to put the sandwiches in* ANNIE's *bag.*

ANNIE *violently pulls or kicks it away from* HAZEL *and flings it across the room.*

LEAVE MY THINGS ALONE.

HAZEL *steps back.*

Looks at ANNIE, *who seems rattled by her own outburst.*

…You think – you think you can treat people any way you want. You think you can just – pack them up like boxes and send them back to the shop. Well, I'm not going back. Richard told me, he said. Why should I go back to nothing?… You have so much you don't even see it. You have everything.

HAZEL *turns to her, genuine, forceful.*

HAZEL. No, I don't.

Beat.

No I don't.

ANNIE. Daniel is my responsibility. I've done a good job. Who's going to get him from school, hmmn? Who's going to meet him at the gates? Who's going to give him his tea?

HAZEL. I'll take care of it.

ANNIE. You'll take care of it?

HAZEL. I'll take care of it from here.

ANNIE. You – couldn't take care of a fly. You're not right in the
head. There's something wrong with you. I've seen. I know.
I know women like you who – put on their hat and lipstick
and say they're going out for milk. I know the kinds of
things you that you could do. He deserves better than you.
He deserves a decent mother.

HAZEL. Well, I'm the only one he's got.

Silence.

…It's so easy from the outside, isn't it? It seems so – simple
when you're the one who's looking in. But you don't know,
Annie.

And the way that people talk and the way they make it
sound. But they don't know. What do they know?

It'll kick in. You just have to wait. That's what they say. You
just have to wait until you – see it. You just have to wait until
you feel it roundly in your arms and smell the top of its head
and – it'll kick in. And there'll be moonlight and music and
you will, by magic, just know what to do. You'll be
enveloped. You'll think of them before you think of yourself.
It's instinct. Animal. You just have to wait.

…Well, what if it doesn't kick in? What if – for some of us it
just – never kicks in? It never feels wonderful, or natural, or
– right. You *don't* know that you would think of them before
you think of yourself. What if every day it seems as if you've
wandered into some – strange forest and the only thing you
know is that you can't get out? What if for eight whole years
you daren't take your eyes off yourself for one small second
because you have no idea what you might do. What if this
was one job you just shouldn't have applied for? Because it's
not in you. It's just not in you. What if that's you?

What if that's you?… You don't know until it happens. But if
it happens… If it happens it's still up to you. You're the
creator. You're the destroyer. You're the mother. It's always
up to you.

Beat.

It's up to me, Annie… And I want you to go.

ANNIE *looks around, desperately.*

ANNIE....I told Richard I'd... And he – promised – He... It wasn't just me who made promises. You don't know the things he said to me.

(*Suddenly.*) *He – wants me.*

HAZEL. Then why won't he answer your calls.

ANNIE *grabs the phone frantically and dials again.*

HAZEL *walks across the room and picks up* ANNIE*'s suitcase.*

There's a bus to the airport that leaves from the station. Goes every hour on the hour. Cheaper than a taxi.

She lays the suitcase down at ANNIE*'s feet.*

There's also a month's wages in an envelope at the bottom.

ANNIE *hangs up – looks at the suitcase.*

It's what you're entitled to. By contract... I checked.

Beat.

I'd take it if I were you.

ANNIE *looks down at the suitcase, then at* HAZEL.

ANNIE. You... never should have stopped being a lawyer, should you?

HAZEL. No. Probably not.

Very slowly, ANNIE *reaches down and picks up the suitcase.*

She takes a last look around the room. Her gaze rests on the knife on the table.

ANNIE. You're going to do something, aren't you? When I'm gone?... You're going to do something to him? You're going to do something to – that?

She points to HAZEL*'s bump.*

Aren't you? I know you. I know women like you... What are you going to do?

HAZEL. It's a girl. Did I tell you that?... No, no, of course I – didn't. Told them not to tell me at first. Had – grand notions of it being a surprise. But then... I asked... A girl.

Beat.

(*Genuine.*) Do you think that that might make it somehow different?

She shakes the idea away.

Never mind. No. Never mind. You go. You – go.

She moves to the door and holds it open for ANNIE.

I don't expect that this is something you'll understand now, Annie. But you don't know... Maybe your poor mother thought she was doing you a favour.

Fifteen

The kitchen. Darkness. Very late.

DANIEL *comes to the doorway in his school uniform, holding a mirror – exactly as we saw him in scene one.*

He walks into the room and places the mirror on the table.

He studies his reflection in it, and rolls up the sleeves of his shirt.

He goes to the cupboard and takes out the first-aid kit.

He puts it on the table, opens it and takes out a bottle of Dettol.

He pours the Dettol onto some tissue.

He brings his ear up close to the mirror and begins to clean it very carefully.

He throws the tissue away. Puts the first-aid kit back in the cupboard.

He drags a chair over to the sideboard.

He climbs onto it and reaches for the smallest knife on the magnetic knife-holder.

He goes back to the mirror.

He looks at the reflection of his ear once more.

Then he takes the knife and slowly begins to lift it.

Suddenly he glances back toward the door as though he is being watched in the darkness.

Nothing.

He turns back to the mirror again and brings the knife to the top of his ear.

He grips his earlobe, closes his eyes and lifts the knife. Then –

HAZEL (*off*). Daniel?

He stops. He lowers the knife. Puts it on the table. She comes to the door.

Daniel?… What are you doing down here?

Silence.

Why aren't you in bed?

The very faint sound of music next door. She goes towards him.

Are they having another party in there? Is that what's keeping you up?… They never stop.

She puts a hand on her bump, absently.

DANIEL. Is it happening?

HAZEL. 'Happening'?

He points to her bump.

Oh. No. She's just kicking.

DANIEL. Hurting?

HAZEL. No. Not – hurting.

Beat.

Here. Give me your hand.

He shakes his head.

Come on.

She takes his hand and puts it on the bump.

Feel that?

He shakes his head.

That?

He shakes his head.

That?

He nods. She watches him.

That's it.

Beat.

It's quiet now. Just the two of us. But in a matter of weeks – in a matter of weeks.

DANIEL. Richard will drive you to hospital.

HAZEL. Yes.

Beat.

No.

Beat.

No, Richard's – busy.

Beat.

Richard's – gone, Daniel.

Beat.

Richard isn't going to be coming back.

Beat.

But I'm here. And you're – here. And… Will you help me, Daniel? When the time comes? You're so good at looking after things. You're so much better at it than me. Will you – help? Will you try? I'll try. I promise I'll… If I – try to be good… will you try to be – good?

[If I… will you?]

He nods.

He takes his hand down from her bump.

She looks around.

(*Re: next door.*) We'll never sleep now, will we? I should get this place cleaned up before morning.

She picks the knife up off the table and casually places it back on the magnetic strip.

They'll be here first thing. That's what they said.

She takes some empty cardboard boxes and puts them on the table.

That's what I think they – said. I never really know.

She starts to place the bottles of olive oil inside the boxes.

Could you pass me those?

DANIEL *passes her some bottles. She puts them in the box.*

And those.

DANIEL *passes her some more bottles. She puts them in the box.*

And those.

She looks out towards the window, the music coming from next door.

…They must have something really wonderful to celebrate next door, mustn't they?

She smiles at him.

He picks up some bottles and starts to put them in the boxes too.

She stops and listens for a moment, trying…

…I wonder what it is.

She picks up another bottle of oil and puts it in the box.

Alone in the kitchen, the two of them carry on filling the boxes, as the lights fade down.

The End.

LITTLE DOLLS

Little Dolls was first performed at the Bush Theatre, London, on 23 October 2008 as part of The Broken Space season, with the following cast:

VICKY	Sinead Matthews
JOHN	John Ramm
Director	Charlotte Gwinner

Characters

VICKY, *the client, late twenties*
JOHN, *the therapist, forties*

…indicates an unfinished or unarticulated thought.

/ indicates an overlap in dialogue.

– indicates a momentary pause or a beat where a thought is being clarified.

A room without light.

An armchair and a straight-backed chair turned towards each other at an angle. VICKY *sits on the straight-backed chair. In the background the loud and persistent ticking of a grandfather clock.*

VICKY, *when she speaks, occasionally struggles for breath. Most of the time she can control it.*

Until she can't.

Silence. The sound of VICKY*'s breathing.*

VICKY. I suppose – I suppose we must have looked like little dolls. Lying there. Each of us in our symmetrical beds, white nighties, faces slightly flushed from the unfamiliar heat. The school had a thing about white nightdresses. They put it on the packing list they sent home to our parents and each of us had bought one specially. I remember mine had a little lace frill along the bosom. I didn't have much in the way of a bosom at the time, but I liked that.

Mrs Lynch said a white nightdress was the marking of a lady. And that's what we were supposed to be. Little ladies. On our best behaviour. And as such we had a uniform.

They – they made us wear our blazers even in the midday heat. Navy and scratchy against the skin. Hideously heavy. Denise in particular complained. But they had her keep it on. We were representatives, not just of a school, but of a country, they kept telling us. Little – ladies lucky enough to see the Monets at the Musée d'Orsay first hand. Little ladies fortunate enough to wander the Louvre and soak up the Seine. Little ladies who would spend ten days speaking French in a place where French was spoken. Not that it should have mattered to eleven-year-olds, but we felt a bit special. We felt a bit golden. We wanted to be good. Do you know what I mean?

Beat.

Well, of course you do. I mean, you do. Of course.

Sorry. I –

She takes a breath.

I'm fine. Where was I? Oh.

Well, I – suppose we got to the hostel some time after
eleven. We had left Paris early that evening and had been
driving for three maybe, four hours in the dark. We were
tired. We had started the journey singing, but – we weren't
singing by the time we arrived. The hostel was pretty. Lots of
wood and watercolours on the walls. A friendly overweight
woman had been waiting up for us – Madame… something.
We could hear the sound of crickets or frogs in the distance
all around – Denise was mimicking them but Mrs Lynch told
her to stop. It was getting on her nerves. Everyone was
cranky with the heat. We each got a glass of orange and a
biscuit and then were sent to bed because of the early start.
They split us into groups of two, six in each room. I took the
bed beside Denise, of course.

Normally, we would've stayed up. Past curfew, you know.
Talking. Or – or eating sweets, or little cakes that we, that we
would've bought when Mrs Lynch or one of the other's
backs were turned and we would've giggled I guess. Little
girls giggle. But that night we were so – after all the
travelling. I didn't brush my teeth. Denise did. And her hair.
She – um – she had lovely black hair. Thick and straight. I'm
sure – I'm sure you've seen the pictures. Everybody
comments.

She brushed it a hundred times before going to bed at night.
Every night. Imagine. I – well – I thought that was great. I
don't think she managed one hundred that night but she – did
as many as she could. And then. Well, then we went to bed.
In our little white nighties. I don't think we even said
goodnight. Our eyes were *that* heavy. Denise had her back to
me. I could see the outline of her shoulders underneath the
sheets and we just – drifted off. You see it was that sort of
place, the hostel. It felt – cosy.

I can understand why the Madame said she never thought to lock the doors.

Beat.

I – I think that's as far as we got – the last time. I mean, I think that's as far as I can go. Like this, you know. I – I've been listening to the clock but I can't quite. I wonder if you could tell me how long it's been? Or should I just keep going? With something else, I mean. I know I'm not meant to stop but it – it seems like we've been here a while and – I'm not counting. I just. I'd like to know. For myself.

Beat.

I'm grateful. For this. Your patience. You're very good. I get the feeling you'd be good, even if I wasn't paying you. Which is nice.

Beat.

I'm sort of embarrassed that we have to do this. Like this. I mean… do you have others you have to do this with? Like this? Others as bad as me? Or are you not allowed to say because of – confidentiality, or whatever. I understand. You just – you must get bored.

Beat.

Are you still there?

Silence.

John?

JOHN. It's been ten.

VICKY. Ten?

JOHN. You've managed ten.

VICKY. Ten. Ten's good, isn't it?

JOHN. Ten's very good.

VICKY. Is ten as long as last time?

JOHN. Last time we did twenty.

VICKY. Oh.

Beat.

It feels longer than last time.

JOHN. It's half the length of last time. Are you alright?

VICKY. Yes. I – Yes.

Beat.

That clock's loud. Was it that loud the last time?

JOHN. I imagine so.

VICKY. Oh. Was it here the last time?

JOHN. Of course it was.

VICKY. Never noticed it before.

JOHN. Do you think you can go on?

VICKY. I think – I think it would help if we spoke about
something else.

JOHN. But you're doing so well. You barely stopped at all that
time.

VICKY. I think – if we keep talking – about this – I'll have to
ask you to put them on.

JOHN. But it's only been ten.

VICKY. I know, but that's really – that's really as far as I can go.

JOHN. Don't forget you have the /

VICKY. I'm trying not to use it.

JOHN. But it's there if you need it.

VICKY. Yes, but I'd like – I'd like not to have to. This time.
Maybe you – maybe you could ask me something else?
Please.

JOHN. Of course.

VICKY. Not about him. I – I don't want to talk about him.

JOHN. No. Alright. We'll talk about something else. Let's see.
Why don't you tell me about your journey.

VICKY. My journey?

JOHN. Yes, your journey here today. Tell me about how you got here today.

VICKY. You know how I got here today

JOHN. Tell me again anyway. Routine is good.

VICKY. My sister collected me. Today. From the flat and drove me here.

JOHN. Your sister – Sarah?

VICKY. Yes, Sarah.

JOHN. And how was that? Your journey with Sarah from the flat?

VICKY. It was – fraught.

JOHN. Why was it fraught?

VICKY. It's always fraught with Sarah. She drives a Fiat. She had to wait for fifteen minutes in the car.

JOHN. Why did she have to do that?

VICKY. Because that's how long it took.

JOHN. It didn't take fifteen minutes last week.

VICKY. I know. It's just. I kept forgetting whether I'd checked, you know. I would get to the bottom of the stairs outside and I would remember that I had forgotten to remember whether or not I had checked all the rooms. So I'd have to go back up the stairs to the flat and I'd have to unlock the door again and unset the alarm again and go into each of the rooms again and check all of the switches again. And I like to turn them on myself so that I have a physical memory – but every time I got to the bottom of the stairs outside, there was always one room I had no memory of at all. Physical or otherwise – So I would have to go back and check and do it all again. And so all in all it took fifteen minutes between the time she sent me the text to say she was in the car outside, to me actually getting into the car. And I suppose – I suppose that would make anyone angry. Really. Wouldn't it?

JOHN. That depends.

VICKY. On what?

JOHN. On what sort of person they are.

Beat.

VICKY. Well. She's big into energy-saving, Sarah. I'm not sure
if I've mentioned that before. She's very 'passionate' about
her carbon footprint. She had those special energy-saving
light bulbs years before anybody else. And sometimes –
sometimes I get the feeling that she thinks that all of this is a
bit of a wilful act on my part. To thwart her efforts. To thwart
everyone's efforts, I suppose. How long has it been now?
Another five?

JOHN. Not yet. You're doing very well.

VICKY. I'm feeling a little bit – I'm feeling a little bit hot.

JOHN. Would you like me to open a window?

He makes some sort of movement.

VICKY. No. No, please don't – move. I think it's better if you
stay where you are.

JOHN. Okay.

VICKY. Thanks. I'm sorry. That clock really doesn't bother
you?

JOHN. I barely notice. Are you alright?

VICKY *breathes.*

VICKY. She's not a bad person, Sarah. I wouldn't want you to
think that. She's put up with a lot. My mother rings her every
week. It's a burden. It isn't like she didn't have enough of all
this 'your poor sister' talk back then. It's not like she needs it
now. She used to say I milked it. The attention. She used to
say that deep down I liked it. Which is a terrible, terrible
thing to say to someone who's lost their best friend, don't
you think?

JOHN. Yes.

VICKY. Unless of course it's true.

Beat.

She – Sarah – doesn't think I should be living alone any more. While I'm like this. She thinks I should go back home. She asked about my bills in the car. Electricity. She asked how much it comes to. She asked how much I pay, like you would ask a person how much they picked their nose. I said not much. But it's all relative. I never turn the television off.

JOHN. And does Sarah know why?

VICKY. Why what?

JOHN. Why you never turn the television off.

Beat.

VICKY. She's not heartless.

JOHN. Of course not.

VICKY. She understands how – I might be afraid. And she – she calls me when thinks I could be afraid, like if she's heard there's a power cut or – something which I guess means she understands why I might be afraid –

JOHN. But does she know of whom you're afraid?

Suddenly VICKY *flicks on a lighter and holds the flame up to her face.*

VICKY. I'm sorry. I just. I wonder if we could maybe have them on now.

JOHN. You don't need them on, Vicky.

VICKY. I think I do.

JOHN. You have that.

VICKY. I can't really see with this.

JOHN. Well, I can see you. I can see your face clear as day.

VICKY. But I can't – I can't feel my heart.

JOHN. Your heart is fine. You wouldn't be here talking if it wasn't. You're perfectly safe, Vicky.

VICKY. I know that. In my head I know that but –

JOHN. I'm here.

VICKY. I know.

JOHN. Nothing can happen here that we don't want it to.

VICKY. No.

JOHN. You have to trust me.

Beat.

VICKY. I do – I do trust you. I just –

JOHN. You just what?

VICKY. I just wish I could remember what normal was like.

JOHN. What do you mean by 'normal'?

VICKY. Normal. You know. Girl, job, boyfriend, flat. Lights on, lights off. Normal.

JOHN. Normal takes time.

VICKY. But I used to be. I used to be completely normal. Long after Denise, I was normal. I used to go running in the mornings. I used to walk in the park. I used to like kissing. If this is in my head… why is it happening now?

JOHN. I think you can turn the lighter off, Vicky, don't you.

VICKY. I don't know.

JOHN. There's a good girl. You're doing very well.

She looks at him, then does so, slowly. Darkness.

Are you alright?

VICKY (*deep breath*). Yes.

JOHN. Your heart?

VICKY. It's – fine. I'm fine. I'm sorry for being stupid.

JOHN. You can go on?

VICKY. I – Yes. I can go on.

JOHN. Good.

She breathes. Darkness.

Perhaps now would be a good time to talk about the message you left.

VICKY. The message?

JOHN. Yes, the message you left on my answering machine last week.

VICKY. Oh.

JOHN. It's been on my mind and I was wondering if you'd care to talk about it?

VICKY. Right.

JOHN. Because, you see, I was wondering what exactly you might have meant by it.

VICKY. Well, I – I didn't mean anything by it, really.

JOHN. Well, you must have meant something by it, Vicky, or you wouldn't have left it in the first place, would you?

VICKY. It was – I don't know – It was a suggestion.

JOHN. A suggestion. I see. And why would you make a suggestion like that?

Beat.

Are you unhappy with the work we've been doing here?

VICKY. No. No. I'm very happy. I'm very appreciative.

JOHN. Because I would assume that if you were unhappy you would have told me?

VICKY. Of course.

JOHN. I would assume you would have mentioned it to my face. I'd like to think that after all this time you and I have built up the sort of honest relationship where you would tell me if what we were doing in this room wasn't working for you. Any more /

VICKY. It is working for me. I'm very happy.

JOHN. So why the message?

VICKY. I don't know.

JOHN. Because, I have to tell you, Vicky, I was a little hurt.

VICKY. Well. It's just –

JOHN. I'm not a piece of wood.

VICKY. I know that.

JOHN. I'm not just an ear, carved into a chair.

VICKY. No, I know. Of course you're not just an ear in a chair.
    You're a – You're a person.

JOHN. Yes.

VICKY. A good person.

JOHN. Yes.

VICKY. You're a man.

JOHN. Yes. I'm a man. In a room with a girl. Sometimes I think
    that's easy to forget. With all this… listening.

VICKY. I don't forget.

JOHN. So why the message, Vicky?

VICKY. It's just – Well, it's just – it's been taking – sort of a
    long time. All this.

JOHN. It takes time.

VICKY. Yes, I know. It does, but… it's been taking longer than
    maybe – I – and other people – thought it would. You know.

JOHN. What other people?

VICKY. Well. I don't know. Sarah, I suppose, my parents, my
    old boss –

JOHN. They thought it would be faster?

VICKY. Yes. Maybe. I – I think they thought I would be back to
    work by now. My old boss certainly thought I would be back
    to work by now.

JOHN. Have you told them that last week you made it to twenty?

VICKY. Well, yes. I have. And they were very heartened, they were *very* heartened, but I... I think they were hoping I would be able to make it through the night by now. Or at least the day. Or at least outside the house. I think they were hoping that after all this – treatment – I'd be – better by now. But – well, I'm not. Not really. I'm still sick. I never have the television off.

Silence.

So, I just was wondering really – when I left the message – if perhaps – maybe we should give it a rest for a while. Or – or have a little gap. You know? Between visits. Because I was thinking – I was thinking that maybe I *should* go and stay with my parents for a bit, for a while even if I don't want to, because it might just be easier because – I might sleep then. But I was thinking that maybe they could drive me up here every two or three weeks you know, for sessions or whatever, if it suited you. If that worked for you. Maybe.

JOHN. So you *do* want to stop?

VICKY. Not stop, no. Not stop, just – maybe... have a break.

JOHN. And do you think that if you have a break he'll stop following you?

Beat.

VICKY *flicks on the lighter. Her hand shakes.*

VICKY. I – I really didn't mean to make you angry.

JOHN. I'm not angry.

VICKY. I'm very happy with the work we've done.

JOHN. I'm not angry. You're my client, I have no cause to be angry with you. Some would say I have no right to be angry with you. But for the sake of honesty, Vicky, and for the sake of clarity, I think I should tell you that I am somewhat disappointed...

VICKY. I didn't want to disappoint you. I just wondered if I
went to my parents if things would maybe be a little –

JOHN. We can't escape our demons by running away, Vicky.

VICKY. I know that.

JOHN. If a man can follow you to London, he can follow you to
other places too.

Beat.

VICKY. But he isn't following me.

Beat.

I mean, you don't think he's following me. And they don't
think he's following me. It's just me that – isn't well. Isn't
that right?

JOHN. Yes, that's right.

VICKY. So. How could he possibly follow me, if he isn't even
there?

Beat.

She holds the lighter up, trying to see him.

JOHN. I can't help but wonder, Vicky, if maybe I have taken the
wrong approach. With you.

VICKY. What do you mean?

JOHN. All this, you know. Five minutes. Ten minutes. Fifteen
minutes. All this easing.

VICKY. I think I needed easing.

JOHN. I was trying to be cautious. But I've been accused in the
past, by women mainly, of being too cautious. It's just I was
sure we were getting somewhere, Vicky. I was so sure we
were close to a breakthrough. I mean, just two months ago
the thought of a room, like this with no – it had you stricken
with fear. And now. Well, now look at you.

VICKY. I know.

JOHN. Look where we are.

VICKY. It's very – I'm very pleased. We've made progress.

JOHN. We *have* made progress. And I'm just. Well, I'm just disappointed that you want to stop before we have really had a chance to – understand all this. And I'm wondering if it isn't my fault in some way.

VICKY. Of course it's not your fault.

JOHN. Perhaps I should've been less tentative.

VICKY. No.

JOHN. Perhaps I should have been less gentle.

VICKY. I'm glad you were gentle.

JOHN. Perhaps I should have been more forceful.

VICKY. You've been very kind.

JOHN. Perhaps, you should give me the lighter.

VICKY. Has it been twenty?

JOHN. Not quite. Not yet, there's still time. Go on, give me the lighter. Let's pick up where we left off.

VICKY. Are you going to put them on?

JOHN. Let's try without them on.

VICKY. I really think I'll need them on. If we're going to pick up where we left off, I'll definitely need them on.

JOHN. Let's just try. Let's just go back to where we left off and try. There's no harm in trying. We might make some progress, we might speed things up. That's what you want, isn't it. That's what your sister and your parents and your boss want.

VICKY. I just want to be normal.

JOHN. Normal girls don't need lighters, Vicky. Now come on. Give it here.

She doesn't move. Her breathing becomes a little louder.

If it becomes too much – I'll give it back. I promise.

VICKY. I don't think I can.

JOHN. Of course you can. We must be firm with our fears, Vicky.

VICKY. I just think it might be better if /

JOHN. I want to make you well, Vicky.

VICKY. I know that.

JOHN. That's all I've ever wanted.

VICKY. I know.

JOHN. But you're going to have to help me.

She breathes.

Now.

Give me the lighter.

He reaches towards her.

Slowly she puts her hand out and gives him the lighter.

Darkness.

So. There you are. In the hostel. In bed, beside Denise. Six of you in your little nightgowns. Like little dolls. Yes?

VICKY *takes a deep breath.*

VICKY. Yes.

JOHN. That's what you said you must've looked like.

VICKY. Yes. That's – that's what we must've been like.

JOHN. And what do you remember then?

VICKY. I – well, nothing. I remember nothing then. I went to sleep.

JOHN. So you didn't hear anything?

VICKY. No. You know I didn't.

JOHN. But let's go through it. So. You didn't hear him come in?

VICKY. No.

JOHN. So you didn't see him?

VICKY. No. I didn't see him. Not then.

JOHN. So you didn't see him, say, as he walked the room? Looking at you all. Looking at you all lying in your beds. Sleeping.

VICKY. No. I didn't. But then, that isn't – what he did.

JOHN. What do you mean 'that isn't what he did'?

VICKY. He – he didn't walk the room looking at us.

JOHN. How do you know he didn't?

VICKY. Because he said. At the trial he said, when they asked him – when he was making his apology to Denise's parents – he – he said he didn't walk the room. He said he just – he just – picked a bed. And went to it.

JOHN. At random?

VICKY. Yes.

JOHN. Denise's bed?

VICKY. Yes.

JOHN. And went to it?

VICKY. Yes.

JOHN. So he chose Denise's bed at random and went over to it. And you didn't hear a thing?

VICKY. No.

JOHN. No creaking springs?

VICKY. No.

JOHN. No rustling sheets?

VICKY. No.

JOHN. No heavy breath?

VICKY. No. No. No.

JOHN. You slept through it all?

VICKY. We all slept through it all. It wasn't – just me.

JOHN. So you were all to blame, is that what you're saying?

VICKY. No. I – I'm not saying – No. No one was to – We were sleeping.

JOHN. You were all to blame because it was dark and none of you heard a thing – is that what you're saying?

VICKY. We were eleven.

The thing is. The thing is – I've thought about this over and over and over. And all I can think, all I can reason is that there was nothing there to hear. And I know that sounds but – I was in the bed beside her. If there was anything to hear I would have been the one to hear it and all I can think is that she – just mustn't have made a sound. She must've – frozen. That can happen, you know, that can really happen. You can be inside yourself, like you and I are now. You can be breathing and thinking and feeling but you can't move. And I – I think that's what – I think that's what maybe happened. To Denise. When he – When she… I think that's why no one woke up.

Beat. She breathes.

JOHN. And what happened then?

VICKY. What do you mean?

JOHN. The next morning. When you went to her bed, what happened then?

VICKY. You know what happened then. I don't think I can do this any more.

JOHN. She didn't wake up.

VICKY. No. I think we need to stop now, John.

JOHN. And everyone was up and everyone was dressing and Denise was still lying in bed.

VICKY. Yes. She was – She was – Her body was sort of twisted but not in a terrible way. It was like she had turned – you know, in her sleep. Towards the door. Her hair – her lovely black hair was covering her face, but there was no, there was no real sign of – She didn't look like she'd been – She was just very still. So I – I called her. I called her name, I said 'Denise, wake up,' but –

JOHN. But what?

VICKY. I'm sorry but I think I need to have them on now.

JOHN. She didn't answer.

VICKY. I really do think I need to have them on.

JOHN. You called her name again and she didn't answer again so you –

VICKY. We must have made it to twenty by now surely.

JOHN. You shook her, didn't you?

VICKY. I can't do this, like this, any more.

JOHN. And what did she feel like when you shook her, Vicky? Just tell me that.

VICKY. I really can't – get my breath.

JOHN. What did she feel like under your hand when you shook her?

VICKY. Please.

JOHN. You've told me this before. You've described all of this before.

He gets up and maybe moves towards her.

VICKY. What are you doing? Please don't move.

JOHN. A dead chicken, you said on your first session here, do you remember that?

VICKY. Can I have the lighter?

JOHN. A dead chicken's carcass. Rigid. Clammy to the touch. Shockingly cold. Do you remember describing her like that?

VICKY. Please will you give me the lighter.

JOHN. Denise. Your best friend. A privileged little lady, in a group of privileged little ladies, who went to sleep in a little white nightdress. And never woke up.

VICKY. Please stop. Please just turn on the lights.

JOHN. There's something awfully beautiful about the thought of that, in a way.

VICKY. You said – you promised.

JOHN. You can almost understand what made him do it.

We hear VICKY*'s breath, laboured and intense.*

VICKY. Please.

JOHN. Almost. All those little breathing bodies. All that darkness.

VICKY. Please. Don't touch me.

JOHN. It lets us away with all sorts of things, doesn't it, Vicky? The darkness.

It presents us with all sorts of extraordinary possibilities. The sort of possibilities one doesn't dare to think about in daytime. The sort of possibilities one could only entertain when one's not watched. The sort of possibilities that, if I let you have this lighter, are suddenly, cruelly, taken away. Do you see what I mean, Vicky?

We hear her breathe.

Your sister, your mother, your boss might think you're troubled. And all of them, I'm sure, are very intelligent people. But the thing I've never said to you before this moment. The thing I wasn't sure I should mention until I got your message on the answering machine. The thing I really feel you need to know, Vicky, is that I don't think you are troubled. You're very, very right to be afraid of the dark. You're right to be afraid of strange men in the street. You're right to be afraid of him. He climbed into bed beside you once, didn't he? What makes you think he couldn't do it again? What's a life sentence in this day and age, anyway?

We hear her breathe.

The darkness is a disease. And you are right not to want to catch it.

Beat.

So.

It's my professional opinion, Vicky, that you are making great strides, but there is more work to be done. You have made wonderful progress conquering your fears. You have faced your past and you have looked at your weaknesses of character with an honesty, truth and integrity that is rarely to be found in one so young. But I don't think you're ready to stop coming to see me, Vicky. Not yet. I don't think our work here is done. I think that would be somewhat – premature. So I am going to give you back this lighter, Vicky, and I am going to turn on those switches, on the condition that you'll rethink your message. I will let you have the light if you discuss this further with your parents, your sister and your boss and come back with an answer that at least makes an ounce of sense. Do you understand me, Vicky? Do we have a deal?

He moves towards her.

We've done much more than twenty today. We've done very well. I think we've made good progress, Vicky.

Beat.

Vicky?

Beat.

Vicky?

He flicks on the lighter and holds it up to her face.

She stares at us, frozen and unblinking.

Vicky?

The clock suddenly stops ticking. He turns off the lighter.

Silence.

Blackout.

Lucinda Coxon
HAPPY NOW?
HERDING CATS

Helen Edmundson
ANNA KARENINA *after* Tolstoy
THE CLEARING
CORAM BOY *after* Gavin
GONE TO EARTH *after* Webb
THE HERESY OF LOVE
LIFE IS A DREAM *after* Calderón
THE MILL ON THE FLOSS *after* Eliot
MOTHER TERESA IS DEAD
ORESTES *after* Euripides
SWALLOWS AND AMAZONS
after Ransome
WAR AND PEACE *after* Tolstoy

Samantha Ellis
CLING TO ME LIKE IVY

Stella Feehily
BANG BANG BANG
DREAMS OF VIOLENCE
DUCK
O GO MY MAN

Vivienne Franzmann
MOGADISHU

Debbie Tucker Green
BORN BAD
DIRTY BUTTERFLY
RANDOM
STONING MARY
TRADE & GENERATIONS
TRUTH AND RECONCILIATION

Stacey Gregg
LAGAN
PERVE

Nancy Harris
NO ROMANCE

Ella Hickson
EIGHT
GIFT
PRECIOUS LITTLE TALENT
& HOT MESS

Sam Holcroft
COCKROACH
DANCING BEARS
EDGAR & ANNABEL
PINK
WHILE YOU LIE

Deirdre Kinahan
MOMENT

Dawn King
FOXFINDER

Lucy Kirkwood
BEAUTY AND THE BEAST *with* Katie Mitchell
BLOODY WIMMIN
HEDDA *after* Ibsen
IT FELT EMPTY WHEN THE HEART WENT AT FIRST BUT
IT IS ALRIGHT NOW
TINDERBOX

Liz Lochhead
BLOOD AND ICE
DRACULA *after* Bram Stoker
EDUCATING AGNES ('The School for Wives') *after* Molière
GOOD THINGS
MARY QUEEN OF SCOTS GOT HER HEAD CHOPPED OFF
MEDEA *after* Euripides
MISERYGUTS & TARTUFFE *after* Molière
PERFECT DAYS
THEBANS

Linda McLean
ANY GIVEN DAY
RIDDANCE
SHIMMER
STRANGERS, BABIES

Conor McPherson
DUBLIN CAROL
McPHERSON PLAYS: ONE
McPHERSON PLAYS: TWO
PORT AUTHORITY
THE SEAFARER
SHINING CITY
THE VEIL
THE WEIR

Chloë Moss
CHRISTMAS IS MILES AWAY
FATAL LIGHT
HOW LOVE IS SPELT
THE WAY HOME
THIS WIDE NIGHT

Rona Munro
THE HOUSE OF BERNARDA ALBA *after* Lorca
THE INDIAN BOY
IRON
THE LAST WITCH
LITTLE EAGLES
LONG TIME DEAD
THE MAIDEN STONE
MARY BARTON *after* Gaskell
PANDAS
STRAWBERRIES IN JANUARY
from de la Chenelière
YOUR TURN TO CLEAN THE STAIR & FUGUE

Lynda Radley
FUTUREPROOF

Nina Raine
RABBIT
TRIBES

Lou Ramsden
BREED
HUNDREDS AND THOUSANDS

Ali Taylor
COTTON WOOL
OVERSPILL

Jack Thorne
2ND MAY 1997
BUNNY
STACY & FANNY AND FAGGOT
WHEN YOU CURE ME

Enda Walsh
BEDBOUND & MISTERMAN
DELIRIUM
DISCO PIGS & SUCKING DUBLIN
ENDA WALSH PLAYS: ONE
THE NEW ELECTRIC BALLROOM
THE SMALL THINGS
THE WALWORTH FARCE

Tom Wells
THE KITCHEN SINK
ME, AS A PENGUIN

Steve Waters
THE CONTINGENCY PLAN
FAST LABOUR
LITTLE PLATOONS
THE UNTHINKABLE
WORLD MUSIC

A Nick Hern Book

Our New Girl first published in Great Britain in 2012 as a paperback original by Nick Hern Books Limited, 14 Larden Road, London W3 7ST in association with the Bush Theatre, London

Our New Girl copyright © 2012 Nancy Harris
Little Dolls copyright © 2012 Nancy Harris

Nancy Harris has asserted her right to be identified as the author of these works

Cover image by Mat Dolphin with photography by Graham Michael
Cover design by Ned Hoste

Typeset by Nick Hern Books
Printed in the UK by Mimeo Ltd, Huntingdon, Cambridgeshire PE29 6XX

A CIP catalogue record for this book is available from the British Library

ISBN 978 1 84842 223 0